Praise for **Tiny Shifts**

"As an experienced couple counselor, Dr. Jake Thiessen excels at presenting common scenarios that most of us have faced and then offering actionable advice and guidance. The concrete examples he provides give us much to think about and even more to act on. As a bonus, there are great illustrations. You will return to this book time and time again, and you will be amazed by the improvements that small changes can make in your primary relationship."

> – **Holly Angelique, PhD**, professor emerita of community psychology, Penn State Harrisburg

"In *Tiny Shifts*, Jake Thiessen takes the complexities of human connection and renders them accessible with remarkable honesty and grace. He connects with the reader in a deeply personal way— as if he is gently holding your hand as you walk through some tricky, hard times, offering you encouragement and clarity.

"What makes *Tiny Shifts* so powerful is exactly that—its embrace of the small, often invisible moments that hold the potential for real transformation. These shifts are not always easy; in fact, they often ask us to look inward, to confront parts of ourselves that we might otherwise avoid. But this is where true growth begins. And when we're willing to do that work, the rewards are immense.

"Each idea is followed by a gentle prompt—'Consider this...' —and there's massive potential in each of them. Whether used as daily insights, journaling prompts, or as quiet pauses for reflection, they carry a transformative power that lingers long after the page is turned.

"Jake's gift lies in his ability to distill what matters most in human connection and to offer language for the things we often feel but struggle to name. Whether you read this book cover to cover or open to a chapter that speaks to a moment you're navigating, it meets you exactly where you are. This is not just a guide—it's a companion for anyone seeking more meaningful connection. With each tiny shift, the world becomes a better place."

   – **Maria Kauffman, CPC, ELI-MP**, career and
      transformational coach

"Jake's wisdom and ability to examine the paradoxes and challenges within couples are profound and hopeful. I have no doubt this book will influence and impact couples on their journey of life together. He is there with the reader throughout the book to lovingly facilitate the journey."

   – **Ford Brooks, EdD, LPC, NCC, CADC**, professor
      of counselor education and director of Growing Edges
      Community Clinic, Shippensburg University

"*Tiny Shifts* is a refreshingly lighthearted yet profoundly insightful guide to the dance of intimate relationships. It explores the underlying currents of connection without ever feeling burdensome, offering a sense of hope, clarity, and validation. I so appreciate the creative format and manageable, digestible approach to this book. While the topics it takes up range widely in scope, they feel very interconnected.

"I thought the world of books on relationships was played and fully realized, but then Jake Thiessen pops this book out. It really hits the mark for my sensibilities—intelligent, deep without being burdensome, with a splash of artful illustrations. A great combo!

"I'll be keeping this wise and delightful book nearby to revisit often—and will gladly recommend it to clients, colleagues, and friends."

– **Laura Beth Moss, CAMS-V, CCIS-V**, NAMA Diplomate, director, Growth Central Training

"If you are looking for practical insights by a seasoned therapist in the business of helping couples negotiate long-term relationships with grace and gratitude, *Tiny Shifts* is clearly a book you want to read. It guides couples who want to work on their relationship to make 'tiny adjustments' to their ways of interacting that can result in greater closeness, intimacy, and understanding.

"This book is perfect for couples and those who work with them. It is one to share with your partner, as it offers ways of seeing and interrelating that can increase communication and engagement. The one-sentence 'Consider this' quips at the ends of the essays offer unique wisdom for couples who want to ponder them and develop their own applications of their meaning and relevance.

"As a lifelong learner myself, invested in a long-term relationship with my husband, I know the stories, advice, and prompts will continue to offer opportunities for our unfolding curiosity about each other that has implications for our growth as a couple."

– **Elizabeth J. Tisdell, EdD**, distinguished professor emerita of lifelong learning and adult education, Penn State Harrisburg

"*Tiny Shifts* is a wise, compassionate companion for couples who want to grow together with honesty and intention. Dr. Jake Thiessen distills decades of therapeutic insight into brief, accessible essays that invite reflection, spark meaningful conversation, and gently reframe relational struggle as part of a deeper, shared journey. Thoughtful and deeply grounded, this book helps couples trade hopelessness for curiosity and stuckness for movement—one small shift at a time."

> – **Cären Rosser-Morris, PhD**, clinical and consulting psychologist and trauma-informed care specialist at Pennsylvania Department of Human Services

Tiny Shifts

Tiny Shifts

Simple Changes to Radically
Improve Your Relationship

Jake Thiessen

Illustrated by Robinson C. Smith

CONTINEO
PUBLISHING

For more information or to contact the author about speaking or about ordering books in bulk, visit www.jakethiessen.com.

ISBN (paperback): 979-8-9990917-0-3
ISBN (ebook): 979-8-9990917-1-0

Editor: Carolyn Bond
Illustrator: Robinson Smith
Book cover design: Robinson Smith
Book interior design: Robinson C. Smith with I Libri Book Design
Author photograph: Marc Faubel, ThatHeadshotGuy.com

Library of Congress Control Number: 2025915169

Printed in the United States of America

*To all the people who have joined me in
the therapy space to learn more about themselves.
In the process, they have taught me
much about myself.*

♥

Chess, which exists predominantly in two dimensions, is one of the world's most difficult games. Three-dimensional chess is an invitation to insanity. But human relationships, even of the simplest order, are like a kind of four-dimensional chess, a game whose pieces and positions change subtly and inexorably *between* moves, whose players stare dumbly while their powerful positions deteriorate into hopeless predicaments and while improbable combinations suddenly become inevitable. To make matters worse, some games are open to any number of players, and all sides are expected to win.

– **Robert Grudin**, *Time and the Art of Living*

One should never know too precisely whom one has married.

– **Friedrich Nietzsche**

Only the paradox comes anywhere near to comprehending the fullness of life.

– **Carl Jung**

Contents

Preface   xix

Introduction   xxi

So, Where Should We Start?

Four Essential Ingredients   2

An Invitation to the Dance   5

The Road Less Traveled   7

Happiness or Meaning?   9

The Importance of Embracing Paradox   12

A Paradox: Separate and Related   14

It's Not That Hard . . . or Is It?

The Most Important Factor in a Successful Relationship   18

Conversation, Not Communication   20

The Sin of Certainty   22

The Art of Listening to Your Partner   24

How to Listen When Your Partner Is Talking   27

How to Talk So Your Partner Will Listen   30

How to Listen When Your Partner Doesn't Talk   33

A Paradox: Mystery and Knowing   35

Is Some of What Happens about Me?

Coming to Terms   38

The Art of Listening to Yourself   40

Make It Interesting   43

Am I Normal?   46

Five Aspects of Personal Awareness   48

Dancing with Your Daemon   59

A Paradox: Special and Ordinary   62

You Think That? . . . Really?

The Truth and the Whole Truth   66

Loving and Lying   68

Incompatibility Is Not the End of the World   70

Thoughts: A Hindrance or a Help?   73

A Paradox: Great Relationships Have an Exit Door   76

Why Do You Always Have to Make It So Hard?

There's No Such Thing as a Stupid Argument   80

A Natural History of Conflict   83

Punctuation   85

Four Ways to Stop Conflict in Its Tracks   87

There Are No Drama-Free Relationships   90

Could You Be a Persecutor?   93

Could You Be a Victim?   96

Could You Be a Rescuer?   98

A Paradox: Sometimes Sacrifice Is Better
than Compromise   100

Is Change Even Possible?

What Comes Naturally   106

First-Order Versus Second-Order Change   108

It's Okay to Try to Change Your Partner   111

Why "Stupid" Topics Create Heated Arguments   113

Going in Circles Doesn't Mean There's No Progress   115

Is It a Spiritual Problem?   117

Are You Stuck or Have You Just Parked?   119

A Paradox: Accept Your Partner to Change Your Partner   121

What Brings Us Together?

Falling in Love   124

Two Fears That Accompany Falling in Love   126

Dancing with Your Lover's Daemon   128

When Sexual Desire and Performance Meet   131

Sexual Accelerators and Sexual Brakes   133

Set and Setting for a Good Sexual Experience   135

Emotion: Neither Too Much nor Too Little   138

Relating to Your Emotions   141

Improving How You Relate to Your Emotions   144

Developing an Emotion Vocabulary   147

Intimacy and Closeness   150

Why Is It So Hard to Stay in Step?

Zero-Sum and Non-Zero-Sum Relating   154

Merging and Separating   157

Pursuer and Distancer   160

A Paradox: Risk and Stability   163

Why Not Make It Simple?

Reciprocity   166

Congruence of Perception   168

Equivalence   170

Understanding Is Not Enough   172

The Need for Control   174

Apologies Aren't All They're Cracked Up to Be   176

Don't Take It Personally   178

A Paradox: Freedom and Limits   180

Why Not Experiment?

The Skill of Not Asking Questions   184

The Skill of Asking Permission   186

The Skill of the Excellent Hug   188

The Skill of the Excellent Kiss   190

The Skill of Encouraging Curiosity   192

What Do You See When You Step Back?

Attending to the Whole of Your Relationship   196

Grounding Yourself in the Present Moment   199

Embracing What Comes Next   201

Afterword   204

Acknowledgments   209

Preface

When I was about fifteen years old, my mother asked if I thought she and my dad should stay together. It was a totally inappropriate question, given my age, but I'm sure she was confused and probably a little desperate. We lived in small town in central Kansas where everyone knew most of everyone else's business, so there weren't many places she could go with that question.

Naturally, I responded with "What? Of course, you should stay together!" She did stay, and I watched my parents work things out over time until they arrived at a good marriage two decades later.

That exchange with my mother, whether it influenced her decision or not, jump-started my interest in couples. Though my life thereafter took many twists and turns, I eventually wound up with a full-time private practice as a couple therapist. The twists and turns included a year in France, two years on a Saharan oasis in Algeria, graduate schools, fifteen years as a university professor, two failed marriages, and the death of a spouse—plus three children, two stepchildren, one foster child, nine grandchildren, two great-grandchildren, and currently a healthy long-term partnership with a wonderful woman.

Long story short, I have learned a lot academically, clinically, and experientially about intimate relationships. For more than four decades I have devoted my career to understanding how couples work and attempting to translate that understanding into useful interventions in the lives of well over a thousand couples. In addition, I've personally lived almost every variation on couple life.

While the claim might sound a bit grandiose, I think I know what I'm talking about.

Because I believe that what one has learned should be kept alive by passing it on to others who might benefit, I've gathered in this book a distillation of insights gleaned while observing couples turn their relationship challenges into meaningful, satisfying connection.

It seems clear that how we treat each other, particularly those we are closest to, goes a long way toward determining how we are in the world and therefore, to some small degree, how the world itself unfolds. In this book I offer practical suggestions for treating your intimate partner with the kind of respect that underpins the world most of us would like to inhabit.

Introduction

"Let me just start by saying: I don't have time for more generic advice that glosses over the real issues—as if we don't already know we need to communicate better or have date nights!"

Those were the first words out of Sandy's mouth after she and Ted had settled into the two plush stuffed chairs in my therapy office to begin our initial session. The two of them spent the next 30 minutes describing their desperation as they watched their 20-year marriage circling the drain. Their intent was clear. They wanted solid, applicable guidance that worked.

I sat back in my chair, allowing what Sandy and Ted were saying to soak in. They were looking for a way to navigate the relentless complexity accompanying the love they still felt for each other. They had tried everything they could find in books, podcasts, and workshops. Coming to couple therapy was their last resort.

In my forty-plus years as a couple therapist, I've seen this scenario often—couples arriving in my office as a last hope.

Intimate relationships are complex. Each partner comes to the relationship with his or her own complicated mixture of learned behaviors, genetic inclinations, and responses to immediate stimuli. They have the task of regulating themselves emotionally and behaviorally. This is difficult enough.

The relationship amplifies the challenge. As two unique individuals join, intending to create a coherent unit that brings stability and satisfaction to each of them, they also need to *co-regulate*, complicating matters further.

Emily Butler and Ashley Randall define coregulation as a "*continuous* unfolding of individual action that is susceptible to being *continuously* modified by the *continuously* changing actions of the partner" (emphasis added).* As the repetition of "continuous" makes clear, an intimate relationship is not a once-and-done situation. It's an ongoing, creative process that when stuck can be agonizing and when flowing can be one of the most beautiful, rewarding experiences life offers.

When a couple encounters a relationship challenge, conventional wisdom says they need to improve their communication and problem-solving skills. Many good books have been written on these skills for couples, and this book offers a few as well. Additional and improved skills are great. But if they are not accompanied by a substantially different perspective on the interconnectedness of their relating, they may simply amplify old, habitual ways of being together. In other words, what they need is a better understanding of the often-subtle effect each partner has on the other and how even a single such effect can alter the direction of an interaction.

They would do well to think of their interactions as a dance where the step one partner takes influences the next step the other chooses. Each partner's steps affect the steps available to the other. The better the partners understand the dance and the more dance moves they know, the more likely their reciprocal movements will lead to connection.

So also in coregulation, the bigger your repertoire of moves, the more fluidly your relationship can progress.

* E. A. Butler and A. K. Randall, 2013, "Emotional Coregulation in Close Relationships," *Emotion Review*, 5(2), 202–210. http://doi.org/10.1177/.

Changing a relationship dance often requires little more than a small shift in awareness and behavior, a tiny yet effective shift that nevertheless may take some practice and courage to apply. Why so? Because changing an ingrained way of relating is not easy. A tiny step applied consistently and with attention to the subtlety of its effect is more likely to produce long-term change than the occasional dramatic step, which is often followed by disappointment.

What Sandy and Ted were really looking for was a manageable, meaningful, immediately applicable intervention—an initial tiny shift—that would begin their journey back to the secure love they once experienced. That tiny shift would then lead to the next tiny shift . . . and the next . . . and the next until they built reliable momentum up and out of that downward spiral and forward again.

If you are looking for that one thing that will solve all your relationship problems, you won't find it in this book. What you will find are suggestions for small steps meant to jog your thinking out of worn, perhaps outgrown patterns and into fresh perspectives and behaviors. The book's approach is existential and experiential, grounded in the idea that new experience is the best route to meaningful change. In other words, less theory, more action.

This book contains nearly 80 short essays grouped into 11 sections by topic. Each essay presents a relationship truth that readers can immediately apply and is followed by a "Consider this" reflection to help personalize the essay's content. These can be used in many ways, for instance, as reflective pauses while reading, as journal prompts, or as ideas to consider throughout the day. Drawings by award-winning artist Robinson C. Smith accompany the essays.

Each essay considers an important facet of relating intimately. Each facet, taken alone, is simple. All facets put together acknowledge the complexity that naturally characterizes intimate relationships.

Most groups of essays end with an essay on a relational paradox, these paradoxes being a little-discussed aspect of relating that can decisively yet unconsciously influence the dynamics of a couple's interactions. Recognizing a relational paradox provides a small yet profound shift that broadens the couple's perspective on their relationship, offering them new options for interacting.

The essays can be read in any sequence. It's not necessary to apply all of them to find a way forward with your partner. Choose the one, or several, that speak to you most directly, apply them, and pay careful attention to the sometimes subtle change that will likely ensue. In much the same way that a one-degree shift in the trajectory of a rocket can dramatically alter where it lands, thoughtfully applying a small step at a pivotal time has the potential for creating radical change in your relationship in the long term.

The book is designed to be read and reread. When you realize your relationship repertoire could use a new move or two, return to the book to find suggestions for change. Even if only one partner in a couple learns and applies the tiny shifts presented here, relationship change can happen. If both partners read the book together, the possibility of change is magnified.

So, Where Should
We Start?

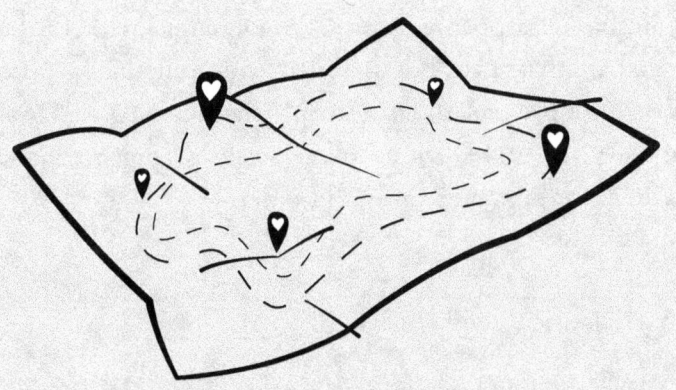

Foundations of a
Rewarding Relationship

Four Essential Ingredients

What would you say is the foundational feature of a lasting intimate relationship? Most people say it's love. Defining love in the broadest way, perhaps that's true. But most people don't define love broadly; they define it particularly as the manifestation of desire: Do you want to be with me? Do you look forward to seeing me and talking with me? Do you want to grow old with me?

Love is important.

So is desire.

Without them, a relationship quickly becomes flat and uninteresting, so you want to cultivate both. But love and desire are to a long-term relationship what an excellent appetizer and a fantastic dessert are to a good meal. Love and desire are necessary but not sufficient.

Here are four essential ingredients every lasting relationship relies on:

Patience. There isn't a couple out there who will say they expect their relationship to be easy. They know there will be challenges. Yet few couples have a grip on what it takes to maintain their commitment through the challenges.

In a word, what every relationship challenge requires first and foremost is a huge dose of patience. The ability to absorb undesirable experiences rather than react to them is the most powerful marker of a couple's ability to weather difficult times.

Balance. Each partner brings a unique set of wants and needs to the union. In a not-so-happy relationship, these wants and needs are often dealt with competitively. This can look like a tug-of-war, with the winner extracting a concession from the loser. Or one partner routinely expresses his or her wants and needs, while the other routinely only responds to the dominant partner's wishes.

In a satisfying long-term relationship, both parties are free to express their wants and needs in an active and ongoing search for balance between them. This looks more like a dance than a tug-of-war. Each knows when to express a want or need and when to listen responsively to a want or need being expressed.

Knowledge. From cooking to carpentry to marriage, all successful creative endeavors require proficiency in skills—knowing what to do and when and how to do it. In a committed relationship, each partner brings a set of relationship skills to the union. Sometimes those skills are extensive and well developed. Often, they are insufficient and shaky.

Learning relationship skills is not all that difficult once you appreciate their importance. If you want to become a great chef, you don't dismiss the value of good knife skills, knowing how to combine flavors, and a knack for beautiful presentation. By the same token, if you want to be a good partner, don't discount the value of good listening, clear self-disclosure, and competent problem-solving skills.

Support. Growing a beautiful rose requires a supportive environment in the form of the right soil, light, and fertilizer. So also, growing a lasting relationship requires a supportive context that helps nourish and sustain it. Sometimes that takes the form of a network of friends and family. Sometimes it's a mutually agreed-upon worldview. A lasting and satisfying relationship is always held by something external to itself.

Love and desire are incredibly important, but they are not sufficient. Without patience, balance, knowledge, and support, love and desire can easily fade, leaving disappointment and confusion.

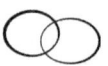

CONSIDER THIS . . .

While love and attraction draw us into a relationship, other factors, like patience and balance, nourish it and make it thrive.

An Invitation
to the Dance

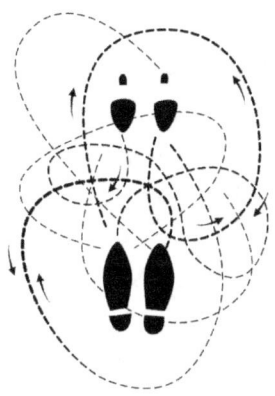

At its core, a healthy intimate relationship is fluid. Its fluid movement is what makes it stable, a bit like what happens when you ride
a bicycle. If you keep pedaling forward, staying upright is easy.
Once you stop pedaling, you're almost sure to fall over.

In relationships, finding stability through fluidity is called
coregulation. Basically, coregulation says that a couple's interactions
cannot be reduced to the behavior or experience of either of them
because each is continually regulating the behavior of the other.
Their behaviors and experiences are intertwined.

This means that what happens between the two people is
more important to the relationship than what happens within
either of them. Said another way, the whole is greater than the
sum of the parts.

Let's take something as simple as holding hands.

Nicole reaches for Chris's hand. Chris responds. That response can be positive and enthusiastic, or neutral and noncommittal, or rejecting and hostile. Whichever it is, how Chris receives that response will influence what she does next, setting off a series of reciprocating responses. That series can flavor, if not determine, what happens over the next few hours and even days.

Most couples have a strong need to identify the meaning behind the reciprocating responses.

For instance, one partner or both might "edit" the sequence. Like a film editor, Nicole can frame the series as starting and ending with certain actions to support her perspective or prove a point. Editing offers a partial and biased picture of the interaction. It tends to result in conflict.

Or Chris might focus only on what Nicole did or said, even diagnosing her ("She is a narcissist"), overlooking her own contribution to the situation.

Trying to understand what happens between two people by editing out parts of their interaction, or by describing the behavior of just one, will always fall short. It misses the intricacy of the "dance" between them that is moving the relationship from point A to point B.

By attending to what happens between you and your partner, you open the door to the information essential to creating the kind of relationship you desire—a fluid and productive dance.

 CONSIDER THIS . . .

Relationship growth occurs between partners, not within one partner or the other.

The Road Less Traveled

Judging from social media posts, magazine covers, and other forms of consumer information, people are looking for an intimate relationship that is exciting, fulfilling, and free of problems—and if problems show up, they can be fixed with a few easy, prescribed steps.

In fact, a vibrant, committed relationship in which the two partners support each other to thrive is as challenging to achieve as it is attractive. The first step is acknowledging this fact, letting that awareness soak in thoroughly, and then diving deeply into the work of making things go well.

Ask yourself if you are willing to explore the patterns operating behind the scenes of your day-to-day relating. Avoiding that deep dive and opting instead for an easier, superficial approach can bring temporary relief if there is a conflict. But in most cases, it also entrenches the patterns further.

It takes a lot of acceptance, patience, and courage to experience the full extent of what is possible in an intimate relationship. Interestingly, it's not just the hard stuff that we resist. Sometimes it's difficult to embrace how good things can be. We sometimes avoid fully enjoying the good parts of our relationship, even unconsciously, keeping our expectations low to protect ourselves from future disappointment.

However, being completely open and receptive to whatever the relationship brings—both the great moments and the challenging ones—is the definition of intimacy. We block intimacy when we limit our emotional experience—when we avoid feeling either very good or very bad.

Intimacy often feels great. But it doesn't always. Even when it feels uncomfortable, genuine intimacy always offers an opportunity for growth.

CONSIDER THIS . . .

If, after repeated attempts, you and your partner haven't been able to resolve a relationship problem, then the problem you've identified is likely not the problem.

Happiness or Meaning?

In my therapy practice, I am often asked questions like "What do I need to do to be happy?" "Why am I not happier?" "My husband/wife isn't happy; what should I do?" These questions reveal the natural desire to replace pain with happiness.

Sometimes the questions probe deeper: "Why is this happening to me?" "What have I done to deserve the heartbreak I'm feeling?" These questions reveal a desire to find meaning in the pain, to become more aware and to grow.

Which is better—the pursuit of happiness or the pursuit of meaning?

I often ask couples, "If you had to choose between a happy life and a meaningful life, which would you pick?" How they answer says a lot about how they approach the painful experiences that are inevitable with an intimate relationship.

Truth be told, happiness and meaning are intertwined. What matters is which one you put first.

Imagine yourself going through a period of relationship conflict and the massive unhappiness that comes with it. Then imagine saying to yourself, "I want to be happy. I can't stand this misery."

What would be your next step?

Very often, the next step is to seek an alternative experience that eases the discomfort and may even inject a little happiness. The worst-case scenario would be turning to the numbing effects of something addictive, like drugs, alcohol, or work. Less dramatically, you, or you and your partner together, might seek distraction by binge-watching a television series or rolling over and falling asleep. Or one of you might say to the other, "Let's go away for the weekend and have some fun." In each case, you would be circumventing the problem rather than addressing and resolving it.

Now imagine the same situation but this time saying to yourself, "I want to find meaning in this difficulty."

What would be your next step?

The next step would be examining the situation with curiosity to discover its meaning. You would ask questions like "How did we get into this situation?" "Where is all this taking us?" "What does the fact that I'm experiencing this difficulty say about me as a person and us as a couple?"

When tough times show up, consider looking for their meaning. Yes, chances are this calls for moving toward rather than away from suffering. However, once meaning is found, genuine happiness is more likely to show up.

♥

CONSIDER THIS . . .

Digging into the meaning of what's happening in your relationship lays a foundation for building enduring happiness.

The Importance
of Embracing Paradox

Being in a committed intimate relationship, like most of life's important experiences, is rooted in paradox. And living in a paradox offers an ideal environment for personal growth, provided you are willing to hold the two sides of the paradox equally.

The concept of relational paradox speaks to the complexity of intimate relationships in ways that most relationship descriptors ignore. A relational paradox consists of opposing stances, principles, or values whose contrast is heightened as two people commit themselves to each other. For example, James and Susan want to be deeply related to each other, *and* each one wants to be a fully separate, self-governing person. The push-pull between these two legitimate stances can decisively yet unconsciously influence the dynamics of their interactions.

Relational paradoxes operate behind the scenes, shaping how the couple communicates and affecting even their most inconsequential exchanges. Because paradoxes are hidden, they are often unappreciated. In most relationships they are overlooked or deliberately ignored. We may be sensing them when we acknowledge that we don't fully understand ourselves or our partner. When reflecting on a particular exchange, it's common for one partner or the other to think, "I'm not real sure what just happened." That's likely a moment when a paradox is at play.

There are multiple relational paradoxes. To examine any one of them is an invitation to set aside either/or thinking (e.g., "I am either happy or sad." "Either this is working or it is not.") and embrace the possibility of both/and, of holding two apparently mutually exclusive stances equally and simultaneously until they reveal a new level of truth. This small yet profound shift broadens the couple's perspective on their relationship, offering them new options for interacting.

Paradoxes hold the broader truths of your life lived in relationship. To miss them is to miss an opportunity to deepen your life. Embracing them is what opens the door to your relationship's deeper gifts.

CONSIDER THIS . . .

Every important aspect of your relationship has two sides. They are of equal value.

A Paradox:
Separate and Related

A wedding is a public demonstration of two individuals joining in a committed relationship. The two people usually enter the wedding venue separately and then literally come together in a bond of relatedness before their friends and family.

Some weddings include a unity candle-lighting ceremony, in which the two people simultaneously light a single large candle with their own candles and then return their candles to their holders still lit. This ritual beautifully symbolizes two individuals joining to become one entity while retaining their individual identities. It also affirms one of the fundamental paradoxes of any committed intimate relationship: being both separate and related.

In each partner there is an ongoing tension between maintaining his or her individual self and becoming an integral part of the relationship. In an intimate relationship both are essential.

It's tempting to avoid the tension by surrendering one side of the paradox or the other. This would mean giving up your separateness to feel more related or giving up your relatedness to feel more separate. Once one side of the paradox is dropped, the integrity of the connection is jeopardized.

Learning to live comfortably with the tension that arises while maintaining both separateness and relatedness is key to a successful long-term commitment.

CONSIDER THIS ...

If you are naturally inclined to want separateness, seek relatedness. If you are naturally inclined to want relatedness, seek separateness.

It's Not That Hard
... or Is It?

Conversation Is Key

The Most Important Factor in a Successful Relationship

What's the single most important ingredient in a successful relationship?

Conversation.

You might be thinking: "Conversation? Really? There must be more to it than that."

Actually, there's not a whole lot more to it than that.

When a relationship, whether between individuals or groups, hits a snag, the cause is usually the inability to exchange ideas in a respectful, open way—the inability to have a conversation.

When two people first get together, there is a lot of talking and a lot of listening—a lot of openness with each other. Discovering that openness is probably why each of them decides to commit to a relationship.

How does a relationship downgrade from a free-flowing expression of interest and curiosity to boredom, distancing, coldness, even hostility? The openness necessary for the free flow of information doesn't suddenly disappear. Typically, it gradually shuts down. The reasons for loss of openness are many and varied, and the rest of this book explores many of them.

Most couples I speak with know intuitively that if they could have real conversations their relationship would feel alive, having the kind of momentum that makes them look forward to time spent together.

CONSIDER THIS . . .

The extent to which you are attached to your own perspective is the extent to which conversation will be difficult.

Conversation, Not Communication

During a couple's first session with me, one of the questions
I usually ask is "What made you decide to do couple therapy?"
Almost universally, one or both partners will say some version of
"We don't communicate enough," often accompanying it with some
confusion, a fair amount of frustration, and/or the implication that
the other person is to blame.

But here's the truth: in a relationship there is no such thing
as NOT communicating. Everything you do communicates
something. Sitting silently with your arms folded across your
chest communicates something. Rolled eyes and heavy sighs
communicate something. Tone of voice communicates. The pace
of talking communicates. Not talking communicates. Throwing
"F-bombs" across the room communicates very clearly.

The notion of not communicating enough is simply wrong-headed. The notion that more communication will, in and of itself, improve things is equally wrong-headed. When couples say, "We don't communicate enough," they are really saying, "We don't have conversations that effectively resolve issues."

CONSIDER THIS . . .

All conversation is communication,
but not all communication is conversation.

The Sin of Certainty

Productive (even fun) conversations are a hallmark of a successful relationship. When thoughts and feelings are exchanged in an easy, free-flowing way, even if those thoughts and ideas are difficult, a couple can feel well-connected.

The one thing that kills easy, free-flowing conversation is *certainty*. For example,

> If Cheryl is certain that being lenient with the kids is right, and her husband, Mike, is also certain that being lenient with them is right, they will "high five" each other and move on. They won't have a conversation. They will simply affirm each other's perspective.

If Cheryl is certain that being lenient on the kids is right, and Mike is certain that being strict is right, they will fall into an argument—not a conversation.

If Cheryl believes in leniency and Mike believes in strictness, but neither insists that their position is the only right one, they are both open to conversation. They can exchange ideas about childrearing and perhaps discover common ground. They can even experience a level of intimacy as they work toward deciding how to move forward together as parents.

The opposite of certainty is flexibility.

Flexibility is necessary for conversation.

Conversation is essential to intimacy.

CONSIDER THIS . . .

Being flexible is a sign that you hold
your views with confidence.

The Art of Listening to Your Partner

In a conversation there are two roles: speaker and listener. While both are essential, I like to emphasize the listener role for two reasons. First, most of us have never been taught how to listen well. Second, listening well has the power to change a relationship. Why? Because it actively demonstrates love and respect in a way that speaking does not.

Listening well creates a safe environment, a nonjudgmental landing place, for whatever your partner is expressing. It's the role that requires the most skill, patience, and maturity.

Here are three suggestions for improving your listening skills:

• Pay attention to the context of your partner's expression. For example, did something happen recently that might be affecting how he or she feels right now?

- Notice your partner's body language and take it seriously. Much of what we communicate is nonverbal. Body language says a lot! Listen to it.

- Speak your partner's words back to him or her to convey that you heard exactly what was said. For example, "You said you are frustrated. I can see that you really are."

How you listen can be very important to your partner, the speaker. Occasionally during a couple session, one partner will say, "When I am speaking, he/she doesn't listen to me. I just want to be heard." My response is to ask, "Do you know how you'd like to be listened to? Can you give him/her some instructions on how to listen, so you feel heard?"

Most people are taken aback by these questions. They haven't considered identifying what they need to feel heard, much less sharing it with their partner.

Figuring out how you like to be listened to requires listening to yourself.

Think about those times when you tried to express yourself and didn't feel heard. Was something missing? Was something happening that detracted from your feeling heard? When you identify what you need, share that with your partner. For instance,

"I'd like you to make eye contact with me when I'm talking about something important to me."

"Please put your phone down when we are talking to each other."

"I'd appreciate you saying back to me what you heard me say so I know you got the message."

Pay attention to how you listen and to how you like to be listened to. Identify exactly what needs to happen for you to say, "I really appreciate how well we just talked through that issue."

CONSIDER THIS . . .

If you don't know how you like to be listened to, there's a good chance no one has ever listened to you well.

How to Listen When Your Partner Is Talking

People use certain stock phrases to convey that they are listening. Using them is considered part of being social and appropriate.

"I hear you."

"I know what you mean."

"I get it."

"I understand."

Too often, these are said out of habit or to fill a gap in the conversation, not from true listening.

To test this, the next time someone says to you, "I understand," ask them to tell you exactly what they understood. They might hit the nail on the head. But if they look at you quizzically and don't know what to say, they were likely hearing you but not listening.

To listen well to your partner, do the following:

• Devote all your attention to what your partner is saying. What you have to say can wait.

• Turn off or put aside anything that might distract you, such as a TV or a cell phone.

• Listen with more than your ears. Pay attention to how your body receives what is being said.

• Maintain eye contact. Don't stare. Do try to convey warmth and receptivity as you make eye contact with your partner.

• When your partner is saying something that seems particularly important, say it back to them. Match their words, tone, and pace as closely as possible. This can feel odd and superficial at first, but important information should be received exactly as it is delivered. Think of yourself as a mirror giving your partner an opportunity to see him or herself exactly as he or she is.

• Take care of yourself as the listener so you can maintain the energy to listen well. Don't let your mate go on and on, especially if you're feeling overwhelmed. If necessary, stop them and say, "I need a moment to take in all that you're saying." Then describe what you've heard and ask if it is accurate.

• Inject your own perspective only after your partner has finished speaking. Preface what you're going to say by asking, "Would it be okay for me to share my thoughts on the subject?" If your partner gives permission, go ahead. If not, remain the listener, even if all you are listening to is silence.

The kind of listening described here takes practice. It is best used for problem-solving and the exchange of important ideas. It may not be appropriate when small talk is called for. Not all conversations are meant to go deep. Some are simply an exchange of observations, like this: "Wow! It's really hot outside today." "It sure is!"

CONSIDER THIS . . .

It's impossible to listen well while anticipating the next opportunity to express your own thoughts.

How to Talk So Your Partner Will Listen

The speaker role has two facets: the content (what you want to say) and the process (how you say it). This distinction is understood intuitively. We react viscerally when someone says something with "attitude"—a case of their process getting in the way of communicating their content.

Choosing your content usually comes first. Part of your job as the speaker is to listen carefully to yourself before you say anything, so you're not just blurting out the first thing that comes to mind. Listening well to yourself prior to speaking brings clarity to whatever you say.

Here are five questions to help you listen to yourself. They align with the Five Aspects of Personal Awareness described later in this book. Your answer to one of them, or several, offers a good entry point for expressing yourself.

What do I think about the topic?

What emotions are generated by the topic?

What am I doing in response to the topic?

What am I sensing about the topic?

What am I intending relative to the topic?

Once you've determined what you want to say and where to begin, be aware of these common pitfalls in of how you say it:

- If you want to make a point that might be controversial, avoid certainty ("I know . . .") and superlatives (best, worst, always, never, etc.). They can make the listener feel anxious and thus less likely to receive your point well. Instead, leave an opening for more than one perspective, which invites the listener to join you in your view.

  Use phrases like "It seems to me that . . ." rather than "You always/never. . . ." Or "I get a little concerned when you . . . ," rather than "You shouldn't do. . . ."

- Be as aware as possible of the emotions behind your expression, as they will color what you say. For example, if you say, "Please call if you are going to be late coming home" with patience and compassion, your partner will likely accept it easily. But if you say it with anger or disdain, it will come across as criticism.

  If you speak from openness and curiosity, a conversation about even a difficult topic will likely go well. If you speak from frustration, anger, or even revenge, it's likely not to go so well.

- Finally, have empathy for your listener. Before speaking, check to see if they are ready to listen in that moment. Do they have the time and energy? Is what you have to say something they likely want to hear? If not, make sure you are grounded enough to say it respectfully.

Expressing yourself well goes a long way toward getting what you want.

CONSIDER THIS . . .

Take your time. The more urgency you feel
to speak, the harder it is to express yourself well.

How to Listen When Your Partner Doesn't Talk

Ordinarily, listening implies listening to something. In a relationship, that something is most likely your partner's voice. But what happens when your partner doesn't talk? Not talking can be the product of anger—giving you the silent treatment. More benignly, it can be the product of temperament—being an introvert. In either case, it becomes important to assume a listening stance even though your partner is not speaking.

Assuming a listening stance when the other person doesn't talk involves self-awareness, imagination, receptivity, and patience.

Self-awareness while listening is complicated. It requires you to be aware of your own thoughts, feelings, actions, sensing, and intentions even as you tune in to your partner's experience and his or her thoughts, feelings, actions, sensing, and intentions.

"But I can't read his/her mind!" That's true, but it's probably less true than you want to admit. This is where *imagination* is essential. The more you genuinely "tune in" to your partner and *imagine* what might be going on within him/her, the more likely you are to accurately anticipate what your partner is thinking.

When you are *receptive* and *patient,* you are more open and sensitive to whatever might show up, no matter how subtle it is. If your partner senses your impatience with silence, he or she may be less likely to speak. When your partner senses receptivity and patience coming from you, he or she is more likely to feel comfortable enough to share what's going on.

Visualize the following scene:

> You are seated on a park bench at the edge of a wooded area. Out of the corner your eye you notice a deer emerging from the woods. If you want to see more of the deer, your instinct might be to turn your head and look at the deer directly. But this would most likely scare the deer away. To see more of the deer, it's better to sit very still, allowing the deer to feel safe enough to emerge further.

The same is true for a partner who isn't inclined to talk freely. Waiting patiently with focused receptivity and attention increases the likelihood of a productive verbal exchange between you.

• • ● ○ ○

CONSIDER THIS . . .

When your quiet attention exceeds your partner's hesitation to speak, the door to conversation will open.

A Paradox:
Mystery and Knowing

The human need to know runs deep and strong. When we know, it's easy to convince ourselves that we have control. And having a sense of control is vital to feeling comfortable.

But most of us also understand that we don't really have control over much of anything. Just watch the news on any given evening. The biggest story is often an event, usually tragic, that unexpectedly turned lives upside down in an instant.

Because humans love knowing, few are comfortable with mystery. Someone might argue that the popularity of mystery novels demonstrates a widespread love of mystery, but what's actually attractive is resolving the mystery. Most mystery novels end with the mystery solved and the reader knowing what happened.

In a relationship, knowing provides satisfaction and comfort, while mystery entices and energizes. Both are needed. For a relationship to remain vital over time, a portion of it must remain mysterious. Mystery is what draws us to the other. It piques our curiosity, invites us to explore.

The duration of committed relationships can seduce couples into thinking there is an end to exploration—that they can know all there is to know about their partner. They may even assume they've arrived at this place of complete knowing, so they end their quest. The relationship then loses energy—and its appeal.

Couples who want ongoing growth and vitality in their relationship naturally seek knowledge about relationship dynamics. They would do well to also cultivate mystery, to embrace the fact that "there's always more here than meets the eye." The interest and curiosity that keep two people actively drawn to each other are fueled by an ongoing effort to resolve the unresolvable. Though this sounds frustrating, it's the kind of frustration that can motivate.

Valuing the mystery/knowing paradox can go a long way toward reducing conflict. When you accept that some things about your partner are fundamentally mysterious, the need to insist on knowing loses importance. As the temptation to believe you know fades, you are more likely notice how knowing limits curiosity and therefore relationship growth.

CONSIDER THIS . . .

Comfort with mystery makes knowing more likely.
Knowing makes mystery more inviting.

Is Some of
What Happens
about Me?

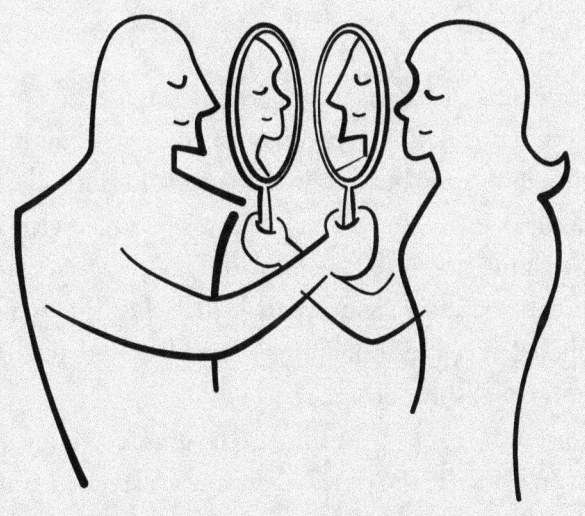

Let's Take a Look

Coming to Terms

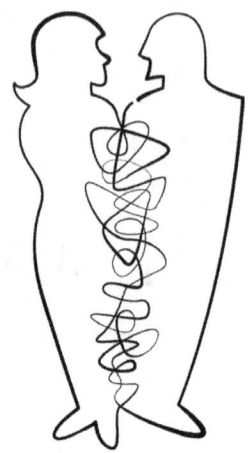

So far, we've looked at relationship itself. However, to create a thriving intimate relationship, you must come to terms not only with your relationship but also with yourself. So, let's take a little time to look at you . . . the individual who's part of a relationship.

Self-examination often begins with cataloging shortcomings and failures because we are quick to notice when things don't go as we hoped. For self-examination to be well-rounded, identifying strengths is equally important.

For instance, notice the times when you've acted out of fear. At the same time, notice the times when you've exercised courage.

Because evolution has hardwired us for caution (anxiety), noting fear tends to come easily. After all, most of us live with a small mountain of concerns . . . some significant, others mundane. Noting courage, on the other hand—the times when you've actually put some "skin in the game"—can be more difficult.

For example, if your partner has been expressing dissatisfaction with your relationship, your self-examination should include acknowledging to yourself that you find this frightening and that you need to muster the courage to address his or her dissatisfaction. You might then find the courage to say to your partner something like:

"When you tell me you're unhappy, I start to think our relationship is in trouble. It scares me. I want you to know that I'm committed to looking at myself and making some changes."

An intimate relationship is to the individual what a competent opponent is to an athlete. Without that "other" there's no real way to come to terms with one's own strengths and weaknesses. If you pay close attention, you get to see yourself in minute detail through both your own eyes and the eyes of your partner. To begin to see yourself through your partner's eyes ask yourself, "What is it like for him/her to be in a relationship with me?"

CONSIDER THIS . . .

Your partner's comments about you are priceless opportunities to come to terms with yourself.

The Art of Listening to Yourself

We don't often think about how we listen to ourselves. We assume listening is something we do when someone else is talking.

In fact, you have a relationship with yourself in much the same way you have a relationship with someone else. And that relationship with yourself—your self-concept or self-perception— is foundational to your relationship with others. So, part of creating a great intimate partnership is listening to yourself carefully and respectfully.

Try listening to yourself the way you'd want others to listen to you. Have empathy for yourself while not taking your thoughts and emotions too seriously.

To listen to yourself, take a step back from your thoughts and emotions to gain some perspective. A bit of distance is needed so you're not caught up in your own energy. (Though maintaining this perspective can be difficult at first, it can be done.)

One benefit of listening to yourself is that you begin to differentiate yourself from others, including your partner. By differentiating yourself you are taking a step toward *having* a self. And the healthiest relationships occur when each partner clearly has a self to offer the other.

If you want to get better at listening to yourself, first acknowledge that you are a complicated, multifaceted being and that the different parts of yourself likely have different points of view. Then listen for these different parts. You might discover something like the following:

> There's a part of me that's angry.
>
> There's another part of me that's confused about why I'm angry.
>
> There's yet another part of me that loves feeling the power that comes with being angry.
>
> There's also a part of me that's embarrassed by how easily I get angry.
>
> There's a part of me that wants to hurt someone when I'm angry.
>
> There's a part of me that wants to protect others from my anger.

... and so forth.

Some parts you may like. Others you may not. Do your best to accept all of them, listening to each one without judgment so it feels heard. Once a part is heard, it can relax knowing that it's been recognized. It no longer needs to clamor for attention. By accepting the less desirable parts of yourself alongside the desirable parts, you accept yourself more fully. This allows you to be more completely yourself in relationship.

Interestingly, you can tell when you're in conversation with someone who's good at self-listening. They talk a bit more slowly and tentatively because they are simultaneously attending to their inner voice. People who don't listen to themselves often come across as trying to convince you of something.

Notice how much easier it is to have a conversation with someone who is carefully listening to themselves than with someone who does not self-listen.

CONSIDER THIS . . .

Listening to yourself gives rise to self-awareness, which gives rise to knowing what you want.

Make It Interesting

I spend much of the typical therapy day listening to couples describe what's not working in their relationships. While some don't know where to start, others launch into a rapid-fire, detailed account of wrongs done and slights endured, laying it all out to me accompanied by anger, sadness, disappointment, and fear.

Once it's all been said, the couple's relief can be obvious. In the pause that follows hangs a simple question:

"Well, now what?"

There is no easy resolution to the months, sometimes years, of conflicts and misunderstandings now identified. Neither partner is likely to have a sudden attack of unconditional love and forgiveness. The road ahead will be winding, hilly, and littered with potholes.

At this point I often ask each partner individually an ostensibly odd question:

"Is any of this interesting to you, or is it just a huge pain in the neck?"

Most people respond by underscoring how awful it all is; therefore, how could it ever be interesting? However, reaching within yourself to find what's interesting about the situation can be a first step toward experiencing something different. Unless you are simply seeking to be entertained, it's your job as a member of the relationship to exercise enough curiosity to overcome judgment and make what is happening in your relationship interesting. This can be a daunting task because it requires coming to terms with the rigidity of your mindset.

Exasperation with the situation doubles the burden and adds nothing to its resolution. Finding it interesting means you've stepped back from it enough to gain some perspective. And a shift in perspective lays the groundwork for a shift in behavior and attitude.

When you're trying to fix an object that's broken, like an appliance or a child's toy, being frustrated or annoyed makes it easy to break the thing further. If you find a way to make the repair job interesting, patience grows. You are more likely to notice details that frustration would have masked. The repair job gets easier, perhaps even fun.

In fact, few things are more interesting to humans than the complexities of relationship. They are the stuff of art, music, movies, even the news. Stepping back from frustration, implementing patience, and noticing the interesting features of the circumstance you and your partner find yourselves in can smooth the road toward creative problem-solving.

CONSIDER THIS . . .

When you make the problem interesting,
you forge a path to connection.

Am I Normal?

Most people, at some point, want to know if they are normal. For many, it's a prerequisite to self-acceptance. The trouble is that there are several definitions of normal.

Normal can mean average. If most of the people on your block are smoking crack cocaine and you smoke crack cocaine, you're normal. If most of them are 60-year-olds with arthritis and you are in your 60s and have arthritis, you're normal. You are conforming to the average life experience in your social setting.

Normal can also mean asymptomatic—if you are symptom free, you're considered normal. So if you have an undiagnosed brain tumor but you're not experiencing headaches or blurred vision, you're normal.

Normal can also mean functioning optimally. In this case, some expert delineates the boundaries of normal functioning. In modern psychiatry, for instance, panels of experts convene periodically to discuss and draw lines between function and dysfunction. If you meet their criteria for optimal functionality, you're normal. If you don't, you're not normal and need treatment.

Finally, normal can be defined in transactional terms. In this case, if you are lying in bed in the fetal position with the covers pulled over your head, crying your eyes out, you're not average because it's unlikely many around you are doing the same. And you are not functioning optimally by any expert's definition. And you clearly have symptoms. But if your loved one died the day before, you're normal.

The next time you find yourself wondering how normal you are, pick a definition of normal and check yourself out. If that definition doesn't work, pick another. Eventually you'll arrive at a definition of normal that relieves you of the unnecessary burden of feeling abnormal. From there you can decide what, if anything, needs to change.

CONSIDER THIS . . .

Realizing you are normal expands your
ability to connect with others.

Five Aspects of Personal Awareness

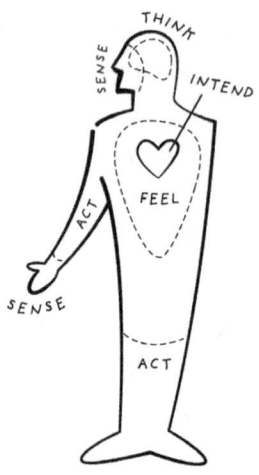

Imagine you are standing in front of the large map at the entrance to a state park trying to decide where to go and what to see. You decide to hike to the falls, but how will you get there? Your eyes scan the map and land on a red arrow that says, "You are here." Ah! Once you know where you are, you can figure out which trail will get you to the falls.

On the "map" of your life experience, personal awareness is like that red arrow. It tells you where you are. It gives you a starting place. Without a clear starting place, movement from where you are to where you want to be becomes chaotic at best and impossible at worst.

There are five aspects of personal awareness: thoughts, emotions, actions, senses and intentions. If you can identify what you are thinking, feeling, doing, sensing and intending, you are fully aware of yourself.

These aspects of awareness are, of course, interactive. So, emotions can affect actions. And intentions can affect actions and consequently emotions. Additionally, senses can affect actions which, in turn, can affect thoughts or emotions. None of these aspects of awareness is static. Movement in any one aspect implies a shift in one or more of the other aspects.

For example, Tim's thoughts about Jennifer suggest a hug would be in order—his thoughts lead to an action that might lead to a specific emotion, such as love. All of that might lead to an intention, such as the desire to make love.

Developing an appreciation for these facets of your psyche and their interactivity will likely positively affect your relationship. The benefits are likely even greater if both you and your partner improve your personal awareness.

Although the following five exercises are designed for you and your partner to do together, you can do them yourself while envisioning your partner next to you in the role of the listener.

These exercises can be done independently of each other. In fact, it's best to not try to do them all in one sitting. Pick one aspect of personal awareness and give yourselves enough time to explore it in depth. These exercises can be done regularly and repeatedly as a way of checking in with yourself and each other.

Awareness of Your Emotions

How you feel matters . . .

In some ways, emotions are the most fundamental aspect of who we are. A newborn's first response to the world appears to

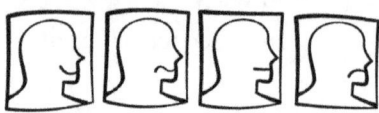 be an expression of emotion in the form of crying. Moving from the warmth and safety of the womb to cold air and a new environment is likely scary. Later in life, most of the time people commit to a relationship based on a feeling: love.

Give yourself and your partner at least 15 minutes together in a quiet space where you will not be interrupted. Sit close enough to hear each other easily and in an arrangement that allows for easy eye contact. Choose one of you to be the speaker. The other will be the listener.

Invite the speaker to complete the following sentences:

- The emotion I have the hardest time with is _____.

- The emotion you express that I have the hardest time with is _____.

- I wish I felt _____ more often.

Once he or she has done this, reverse roles.

After both of you have completed the sentences, take a few minutes to converse about the emotions each of you just identified.

- Did you name the first emotion that came to mind, or did you give yourself time to dig deeper?

- If you were to do the exercise over, would you say the same things? If not, what would you say instead?

- As the listener, did you hear what you expected or were you surprised?

After completing the exercise, thank each other for taking the time to share and to listen.

Awareness of Your Thoughts

How you think matters . . .

It's not an accident that positive thinking is a popular topic for self-help books. How you think about yourself, your partner, and life in general colors how you move forward.

Give yourselves 15 minutes together in a quiet space where you will not be interrupted. Sit close enough to hear each other easily and in an arrangement that allows for easy eye contact. The one who went second last time goes first this time.
Complete the following sentences:

- Right now, I'm thinking _____ about our relationship.

- The thought that most encourages me about our relationship is _____ .

- I wish I didn't think _____ about our relationship as often as I do.

- I commit to thinking positively about our relationship. The positive thought that I want to hold in my mind is _____.

Once he or she has done this, reverse roles.

After both of you have completed the sentences, take a few minutes to converse about the thoughts you've just identified.

- What is the effect of holding negative thoughts about your partner or the relationship?

- What kind of thoughts would you like to hear your partner share?

- When you do think positive thoughts about the relationship, is there something that keeps you from expressing them?

After completing the exercise, thank each other for taking the time to share and to listen.

Awareness of Your Actions

How you act matters . . .

"Actions speak louder than words." Being aware of your actions and their implications helps you understand the effect you have on others. This sounds easier than it is because while we may be aware of our actions, we often miss how those actions affect others.

To increase awareness of actions and their implications, imagine watching yourself on a screen. This will help you see yourself  objectively. You may notice that many of your actions are habitual and done unconsciously. If you then consider your partner's responses to what you are doing, you will begin to see the impact of your actions.

Give yourselves 15 minutes together in a quiet, uninterrupted space. Sit close enough to hear each other easily and in an arrangement that easily allows for eye contact. Whoever went second last time goes first this time.

Complete the following sentences:

- The thing I do in our relationship that I wish I didn't do is _____.

- The one thing I wish you would do for me is _____.

- If I started to do _____ I believe our relationship would improve.

- There's something in me that stops me from doing positive things. That something is _____.

Once one of you has done this, reverse roles.

After both of you have done the exercise, give yourselves a few minutes to converse about the actions or lack of actions you've just identified.

- What were you feeling when you listened to your partner?

- What excuses do you employ to not act positively toward your partner more regularly?

- Do you "keep score"? If so, what effect does that have?

After you've completed the exercise, thank each other for taking the time to share and to listen.

Awareness of What You Are Sensing

What you sense matters . . .

What you sense can be physical (hunger, fatigue, pain) or more subtle (unease about money, discomfort about how the day is going, the relaxation that comes with good news).

What you sense, physically or otherwise, is a felt experience—how you are in your body in a given moment or with a particular person, issue, or event. That felt sense shows up automatically before thoughts or emotions. (It is not as straightforward as awareness of your emotions, thoughts, or actions and may take a little time and patience to get used to.)

For example, when meeting someone for the first time, you may have a sense of ahhhhh! (positive) or ugh! (negative). Sometimes people refer to what they're sensing as a "vibe." "I just got a really good vibe about her." Or "He left me with a really bad vibe."

Many exchanges between partners are prompted by subtle sensing. Notice how often questions arise like "Why did you do that?" or "Why did you say that?" The response is often "I don't know." However, paying close attention to subtle sensing can offer a clue as to why something was done or said—for instance, "Something in me sensed your agitation."

Give yourself and your partner 15 minutes together in a quiet space where you won't be interrupted. Sit close enough to hear each other and in an arrangement that allows for easy eye contact.

Sit quietly for a minute or two, each of you simply noticing how you are in your body. Then choose who will speak first.

Complete the following sentences:

- When I consider myself right now, the felt sense I have is _____.

- When I consider our relationship right now, the felt sense I have is _____.

- My sense of the strength of our relationship is _____.

In our relationship, I frequently sense _____.

- The felt sense I get when I think about our future is _____.

Once one of you has done this, reverse roles.

After both of you have completed the exercise, give yourselves a few minutes to converse about the things you've each identified.

- How difficult or easy was it to identify a felt sense about yourself? About your relationship?

- Were you able to notice how your felt sense wants you to move forward?

- How easy or difficult was it to hear your partner's description of his or her felt sense?

After you've completed the exercise, thank each other for taking the time to share and to listen.

Awareness of Your Intentions

What you intend matters ...

Intentions are about the future. They express desires or wants, providing a compass that tells you where to go next. Knowing your intentions and sharing them with your partner reveals a path the two of you can thenconsider to get from where you are to where you'd like to be.

Give yourselves 15 minutes together in a quiet, uninterrupted space. Sit close enough to hear each other easily and in an arrangement that allows for easy eye contact. Whoever went second last time begins this exercise.

Complete the following sentences:

- When I think about my own personal growth, I intend to _____.

- When I think about us, about our relationship, I intend to _____.

- For me, the future is _____.

The one thing about the future that concerns me the most is _____.

- The one thing about the future that gives me the most comfort is _____.

Once one of you has done this, reverse roles.

After both of you have done the exercise, give yourselves a few minutes to converse about the intentions you've just identified.

- Did you find yourself saying things that were reassuring to one or both of you?

- Or did you find yourself saying things that felt uncomfortable—maybe anxiety provoking?

- What do you notice about how you think of the future and your relationship?

- How has your sense of the future shifted, even if slightly, over the past week?

   After you've completed the exercise, thank each other for taking the time to share and to listen.

Dancing with Your Daemon

David, like most people who want to be a good partner, has had his share of unpleasant conversations with his partner, George, about where he falls short. In a session he recalled one such conversation:

It feels like it happened yesterday. George described me as frightened. The idea that I was fearful was so thoroughly outside my consciousness that I took offense. Defending myself, I said I'd successfully navigated all kinds of tough situations, so how in the world could I be fearful?

It's painful to recall that conversation because it showed how poorly I understood myself at the time. Now I see how much energy I put into defending myself when I really needed to acknowledge the truth that many of my decisions and much of my behavior were rooted in fear. I was afraid of being vulnerable and of disappointing George. I have since learned that fear is my daemon.

The idea that we each have our own unique daemon has been around for a while. Carl Jung referred to it when he identified the shadow part of us as important and influential. The Enneagram, a personality typing system, considers it as central to how we approach our lives. Fantasy novelist Philip Pullman, in *His Dark Materials* trilogy, externalizes his characters' daemons as intelligent beings in animal form that are a vital part of how the characters grow and relate.

"Daemon" refers to basic tendencies of temperament and personality that underlie how a person thinks and much of what they do. When you think of someone as "laid-back" or "hotheaded," you are usually pointing out their daemon.

Steven Pinker, in *The Blank Slate: The Modern Denial of Human Nature*, is referring to the daemon when he says there are fundamental parts of us that can't be changed by our environment. We were born with traits (daemons) that stay with us no matter what we do. You can alter these traits to some extent, but they can't be eliminated.

It's naïve to relate to yourself or others without acknowledging that something powerful is operating beneath or alongside the obvious. It's like assuming a tranquil, free-flowing river has no power to become a raging torrent under the right conditions.

Coming to terms with your daemon, recognizing the strengths and weaknesses it brings, is fundamental if you want your relationship to have the kind of integrity necessary for it to thrive. You can't ignore who you are and what it is that "makes you tick."

The more you are willing to acknowledge your daemon and explore it, the more you have to offer to your intimate partner. Knowing your daemon and relating well with it leads to deeper conversations and new avenues for relationship growth.

For David, discovering that fear is his daemon helped him understand why he so easily reacts to George. Once aware of his daemon, he can better identify occasions when he needs to take the reasonable risk of putting aside his fear in favor of openness.

CONSIDER THIS . . .

Knowing what about you can't change makes it easier to identify what can change.

A Paradox: Special and Ordinary

Humans are complicated.

As much as we may want to be normal, we also want to feel completely special. The dialectic between ordinary and special resides at the core of intimate relationships, yet it often goes unacknowledged.

The longing to feel special makes sense, given the high value our culture places on self-esteem and uniqueness. And yes, everyone has worth simply for being the specific human being they are. But it's equally true that everyone is quite ordinary.

Ordinary is what connects you to others because ordinary guarantees similarity of experience. If you were completely unique, you would have too little in common with others to generate a connection. Paradoxically, one of the most complimentary things you can say about someone who seems special—a celebrity, for example—is "He/She is so down-to-earth." The famous person's ordinariness makes it easier for you to relate to him or her.

You may think that if your partner would just make you feel special, the two of you would feel more connected, since when you feel special, you feel valued. Yes, both you and your partner need to feel valued.

But is feeling special what makes you feel connected?
Good question!

Receiving an unexpected and thoughtful gift can make you feel special. Crawling into bed with your life partner after a long day is completely ordinary. Which one creates the stronger sense of connection?

CONSIDER THIS . . .

The route to real connection runs through ordinariness.

You Think That?
....Really?

Dealing with Differences

The Truth and the Whole Truth

When a relationship crisis arises, it injects a huge dose of fear into both partners. The antidote to that fear, in most people's minds, is the truth. They say things like "If he would just tell me the truth, I think we could work this out." Or "If I knew what's really going on, I could deal with it."

However, in the rush to manage the fear, one partner may latch on to a specific truth and interpret it as the whole truth.

For example,

Bill picks up Susan's phone, mistaking it for his own, and notices that a mutual male friend of theirs has phoned Susan three times in the past hour but hasn't left a message. Suddenly he is afraid—can he still trust Susan?

To get to the truth, he chooses a good moment and says, "I glanced at your cell phone, and I saw that Malcolm called you three times within an hour today." That their friend phoned her three times in short succession is true. Bill rightfully wants to know what it means. He then says, "It makes me wonder if there's something going on between you and Malcolm."

In his anxiety about his relationship with Susan, he has leaped to a conclusion. He would do better to recognize that the suspicious action is only *a* truth and remain calm and steady until *the whole* truth has a chance to emerge.

The whole truth might be that Susan and Malcolm are planning a surprise birthday party for Bill. Or that Susan has felt lonely and isolated lately because Bill has been preoccupied with his work, so she reached out to their friend for comfort. In either case, the whole truth, once revealed, adds important information to the situation.

Refraining from jumping to conclusions takes patience, as well as courage and compassion. A good way to access patience, courage, and compassion is to recall what made you fall in love with your partner and remember that those features are still a part of him/her. Another important antidote to jumping to conclusions is to remind yourself of your own resilience.

CONSIDER THIS . . .

You can't get a grip on the whole truth
when you are holding tightly to a partial truth.

Loving and Lying

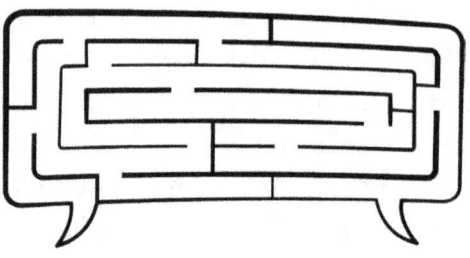

We say we value honesty. We say it's essential to a successful relationship. But we lie to each other and ourselves with amazing regularity.

In its most benign form, we lie to protect "good" secrets—like what's in the package under the Christmas tree or "You really don't look all that great this evening."

Children lying to their parents is considered a necessary step in their quest for independence. For example, when your father knocks on your bedroom door asking, "What's all the commotion in there?" what do you say? Most likely "Nothing!" You don't say, "Well, Dad, truth be told, I'm dancing naked in front of my mirror because it feels good." In fact, it's none of his business what's going on if it's legal and moral, so you spare yourself and your dad the unpleasantness of saying, "It's none of your business what's going on in here" and just say, "Nothing." And both you and he know it's a lie.

In a healthy family there's space for this kind of "dishonesty." Everybody accepts it for what it is, and no one is offended. It's said that if you can't lie, you can't leave home.

In its destructive form, lying creates a gulf between two people that quickly widens. Like a wildfire, "You're lying" can quickly expand to "You're a liar." On principle, once you've arrived at "You're a liar," conversation is all but useless. How can you have a productive, reliable conversation with a liar? You can't. Everything is suspect when you're dealing with someone you've labeled a liar.

Yet lying is such a common human behavior that we often find ourselves bound to people we've at some point considered "liars," whether their lies were benevolent or destructive. Deciding not to communicate with our spouse, our child, our landlord, our banker is impractical. We must maintain a level of openness if for no other reason than basic life efficiency.

How do we navigate this treacherous terrain?

One way is to recognize that lying is all about self-protection.

If I believe my spouse is lying, my first job is to make sure he or she has no good reason to be self-protective—that I'm not on the attack and thus giving him or her a reason to be self-protective. This can be a difficult task if I am deeply suspicious about my partner's behavior.

Most lying is a product of caution, even fear. It follows, then, that if you don't want your partner to lie to you, make sure he or she feels safe enough to tell the truth. More than dealing with a person who's lying, you're dealing with a person who's frightened. Much more than the dishonesty, it's the fear that deserves attention.

CONSIDER THIS . . .
It's possible to take lying too seriously.

Incompatibility Is Not the End of the World

According to most of the research on relationship success, compatibility between partners is essential. If two people have, for instance, the same definition of "clean," the same definition of "on time," and the same definition of "expensive," they are more likely to be compatible and less likely to experience conflict.

But what about "hardwired" differences like those that come with temperament and personality or with being male or female? What about the natural inclination for opposites to attract? And what about the innate desire to encounter something new and interesting—something unlike you—that adds life and spark to a relationship?

No matter how much we seek compatibility, we are going to find pockets of incompatibility as the relationship develops. Those points of incompatibility sometimes generate gnawing disappointment, but they can also create interest and curiosity.

If allowed, they can be sources of substantial personal and relational growth. Though it's a cliché, pain and gain are indeed tied to each other.

Couples seek therapy almost always because of a pointed and painful experience of incompatibility. As they describe what's going on, it quickly becomes obvious that at an earlier point in their relationship their differences were experienced as sources of interest and growth, not pain.

What turns something that once generated interest into something that produces annoyance and frustration? Here are three possible causes.

- The loss of imagination and curiosity that comes with a long-term relationship.

- The diminished emotional space for navigating differences that happens as responsibilities like children and mortgages accumulate.

- The natural erosion of respect that occurs as disappointments and misunderstandings, both small and large, pile up and acquire weight.

How, then, do you deal with incompatibility (assuming it's not creating a dangerous situation)? Here are three possible responses.

- Cultivate imagination and curiosity. Ask yourself, "What makes him/her do that?" or "How does doing that work for him/her?" or "How does my response make him/her more (or less) likely to continue doing the thing I find annoying?"

- Look for ways to create constructive emotional space that allows for differences. One way is to remind yourself that your partner is not doing something to you. For example, if I walk in the kitchen and see my partner rearranging the dirty dishes in the dishwasher after I've already placed them there, she is not doing something to me; she's doing something for herself.

- Increase the level of respect. This can be done most easily by paying attention to how you hold your perspective on the topic of the moment. If you hold your perspective in an angry or defensive way, your partner will be less likely to respect you than if you hold it while embracing the fact that he or she may not agree with you.

Of course, this is easier said than done. Most people at some point find themselves wishing their partner were more like them, not less. This longing for similarity over difference is completely normal. When differences seem overwhelming, reminding yourself that growth comes only with risk and difficulty can move you from discouragement to hope.

CONSIDER THIS . . .

Incompatibility is the space between two people where growth can happen.

Thoughts: A Hindrance or a Help?

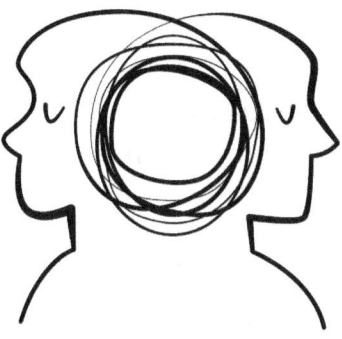

Cory "drives truck." It's what his dad did for a living, and it's what he fell into doing after graduating from high school. He dated Cindy, an x-ray technician at the local hospital, for two years before they decided to get married. All went well until they realized they needed more income. So Cory took a job driving a truck over the road, which meant he was away from home for days at a time.

The additional money was nice, but the change in Cory's work-life pattern had its effect. While he was on the road, he and Cindy texted frequently, called when they could, and tried to video chat every night before bed. Still, driving gave Cory a lot of time to think, and evenings at home alone gave Cindy a lot of time to think as well—memories of doing things together, from walks around their neighborhood to good times with friends to amazing sexual encounters.

Gradually, their thoughts began to generate suspicion. Cory found himself wondering about the relationships Cindy had developed at the hospital. Was she chatting with her single friends about being able to go out and have a good time without worrying about what her husband would say? He knew she could be flirtatious. Was she flirting with some of the guys she worked with?

Cindy found herself wondering how Cory spent his nights. Did he really sleep in his truck? Was he developing relationships with people at his regular stops? What about the women who troll truck stops looking to make a few bucks by giving truckers some "companionship."

So many thoughts!

Fridays around five o'clock, when he usually arrived home, was Cory's favorite time of the week. The same was true for Cindy. She could hardly wait for the end of her shift on Fridays. Yet they both began noticing that their reunions were marred by an inexplicable hesitation. Sure, they hugged and gave each other a kiss, but they didn't run into each other's arms like they used to.

Each one's thoughts were taking a subtle yet real toll, like a subtly negative force field forming between them—not so strong that they argued but strong enough to make them drift slightly apart.

One Saturday night after they'd had a couple of drinks Cory found himself asking Cindy, "What are you thinking?"

The alcohol prompted her to speak with more candor than usual. "Sometimes my thoughts keep me awake at night. I lie there wondering what you're doing at that moment—I mean what you're really doing. I get these racing thoughts that take me to places I don't really want to go and that I even think are a little crazy."

Cory smiled ruefully. He leaned toward her and said, "You know, I have those same thoughts more nights than I wish. I wonder about what your life is like when I'm not around."

Thoughts help to frame our experience, giving it a direction. Sometimes that direction is good. Other times it can be disastrous.

Cory and Cindy were becoming aware of their own and each other's thoughts. Sharing this awareness in a nonjudgmental environment let them clear up doubts and put the relationship back on a solid footing.

CONSIDER THIS . . .

Treat your thoughts as you would treat someone you've just met . . . be curious and be cautious.

A Paradox:
Great Relationships
Have an Exit Door

There are few decisions weightier than the decision to marry, to remain together until "death do us part."

In fact, the couple not only wants to remain together; they want the vibrancy of their original decision to marry to continue unabated throughout the life of the marriage. However, a satisfying and secure relationship rests upon a foundation of ongoing choice. And choice always introduces a measure of anxiety.

Consider these two scenarios:

Scene One

The big day arrives. Friends and family gather. The bride walks up the aisle and is greeted by her groom. They exchange vows and are pronounced married.

Together they walk back down the aisle and into the beautifully furnished space that constitutes their marriage.

They close the door behind them, lock it, and pitch the key out of reach, determined to remain together forever.

Every day thereafter, they get up in the morning and say, "I love you. I choose you." The "I love you" is clear and true in the moment. But the "I choose you" cannot be true in the moment because they chose each other once, then pitched the key out of reach and called it done. They opted for the security that comes with removing choice.

Scene Two

The big day arrives. Friends and family gather. The bride walks up the aisle and is greeted by her groom.
They exchange vows and are pronounced married.

Together they walk back down the aisle and into the beautifully furnished space that constitutes their marriage. They close the door behind them, lock it, and each put a key in their pocket.

Every day thereafter, they get up in the morning and say, "I love you. I choose you." Both the "I love you" and the "I choose you" are true in the moment because each partner has a key to the exit door—each retains the freedom to make a choice.

A guaranteed way to snuff out the fire of love and desire is to deprive it of the oxygen that freedom to choose provides.

Here's an example of the same paradox with respect to a different choice:

Craig and Melanie chose to live near Melanie's family because they wanted her family's support in raising children. Craig was just offered a promotion that would require moving away to a larger city. Both Craig and Melanie are painfully aware that the new job offers an "exit door." Craig could exit the marriage, or Craig and Melanie could exit their life close to her parents.

They could respond by saying, "No, we can't make a change. We are committed to the marriage, the kids love their grandparents, and we can't be without that support. Let's not even wonder about alternatives." End of story. In this case, they threw away the key on this choice back when they decided to live where they are now.

Or they could embrace the choice before them, delve into its drawbacks and possibilities, and make a new choice born of openness and careful consideration.

The first response eliminates the fact that Craig and Melanie are actually free to exercise choice in every moment. The second embraces the reality of choice and, whichever option they decide on, leaves the couple feeling in charge of their life together.

A resilient long-term connection requires fresh air, the right amount of space, and a clearly marked exit. Its viability depends on being able to look around and say with conviction, "I'm here now because I choose to be here, not because I made a choice months (or years) ago and gave up my freedom."

CONSIDER THIS . . .

A trap has no exit. For freedom and love
to thrive, an exit must be present.

Why Do You Always Have to Make It So Hard?

Conflict and What to Do about It

There's No Such Thing as a Stupid Argument

When a couple decides to seek professional help, it's usually because they've come to the end of what they can do for the relationship on their own. Often, it's because they've been arguing unproductively. And often the first session starts with one of them saying, "We just keep having stupid argument after stupid argument. We can't seem to get out of the loop."

Thankfully, I'm no longer tempted to ask about the topic of their discord. Instead, I say, "There's no such thing as a stupid argument. There are plenty of stupid topics, but there's never a stupid argument."

Just as every cell contains the DNA of the organism, every encounter, especially a negative encounter, contains the DNA of what's really going on between the two partners. Arguments, no matter the topic, always revolve around some crucial dynamic in the relationship.

Sometimes the argument points to problems of power or control:

Who is in charge? Who gets to decide what happens next?

Sometimes it points to quality of attachment:

Do you really love me? Will you stay with me?

Sometimes it is about fear that the other person isn't being open and honest:

I don't know if I can trust what you're saying.
It feels like more is going on than meets the eye.

The more a couple focuses on an argument's topic, the less likely they are to resolve what's really fueling it. It takes self-discipline and insight to look past the topic of the exchange and attend to the relationship dynamic underlying the argument.

Next time you find yourself and your partner in the middle of a "stupid" argument, ask yourself: "What's really going on here? What is driving this unproductive fight? What might be the deeper conflict we are really trying to resolve?"

Asking these questions will shift your focus from the topic to the underlying cause.

An example:

Every Saturday when they set out to do the grocery shopping, Katy and Jeff feel the discomfort of their differences. They are committed to doing things like shopping together because they genuinely enjoy each other's company—most of the time. But Katy is all about organic foods and eating healthy, while

Jeff worries about money. Every time Katy reaches for organic produce, Jeff thinks, "Why are we spending all this money on organic when we could just get the basic lettuce at half the price?" So they have an argument about, of all things, lettuce.

At play underneath their bickering, however, is the relational paradox of freedom versus limits. Jeff is afraid of freedom. He's afraid that Katy's freedom with spending money will leave them in a financial bind. He thinks: "Lettuce is just the beginning. If she has her way, we'll wind up buying an over-priced electric car just because she wants to save the environment."

Katy, on the other hand, is afraid of limits. She doesn't want to be told she can't spend money on something she defines as important. She thinks: "Why does he always have to block me when I'm trying to do something good for us? Can't he see how I'm trying to make things better?"

Lettuce—it's a stupid topic for an argument, but the argument itself is far from stupid. It's rooted in deeply held perspectives that are rarely acknowledged.

CONSIDER THIS . . .

Given the opportunity, the inner workings
of a relationship will always make
themselves known.

A Natural History of Conflict

There's a natural, three-stage progression to conflicts.

Stage one—the issue. Ordinarily, a conflict begins with one partner attacking what the other partner has identified as an issue. For example, a wife might say to her husband, "It really bothers me that you leave your dirty socks for me to pick up and deal with."

If her husband responds by addressing the issue—for example, if he were to say, "I'm sorry, I get distracted and don't pay attention to what I'm doing"—the conflict will go no further.

Stage two—the person. If, however, he chooses to ignore her concern, in frustration she will likely progress from attacking the issue to attacking the person. She might say, "I've asked you several times to clean up your dirty socks, and you won't do it. You're such a slob!"

Sometimes this escalation prompts the change she wants to see. He might say, "I'm sorry, I didn't realize it was that important to you. I'll pick them up." More often, however, the attack prompts defensiveness in the form of a counterattack: "Well, picking up socks is no big deal compared to how crappy you leave the car looking. Talk about being a slob!"

Stage three—the relationship. When attacking the person fails to generate the desired change, the conflict may shift to stage three: attacking the relationship. The wife might say something like, "I've asked you repeatedly to clean up after yourself. But no, you're too lazy. I can't live like this anymore. This relationship isn't what I signed up for."

When a disagreement arises, keep the focus on the issue. If the conflict progresses to attacking each other or the relationship, the issue gets clouded with fear and hurt and becomes even more difficult to resolve. If this continues fight after fight, the bond between the partners will eventually weaken, eroding the foundation of the relationship.

CONSIDER THIS . . .

Any escalation beyond addressing the issue at hand is aggression.

Punctuation

Consider these two sentences:

A woman without her man is nothing.

A woman: without her, man is nothing.

Clearly, punctuation matters!

It's not only the meaning of a sentence that is shaped by punctuation. History is shaped by punctuation too. Listen to any couple arguing and you will notice they spend a good bit of time going over historical events. These events don't have to be in the distant past. In fact, most arguments are about events in the recent past—sometimes the very recent past.

Here's an example:

Ken: "Last night, I was just sitting there enjoying some down time, minding my own business, when out of the blue you laid into me. It's like you were looking for a way to make me feel bad."

Judy: "Out of the blue? You've got to be kidding! I've asked you a dozen times over the past couple of days to pay the electric bill. What's happened? Nothing! So today we got a shut-off notice."

Ken: "Well, I asked you yesterday if there was enough money in the checking account to pay the bill. You acted as if you didn't hear me. I would have paid it if you had just told me we had the money."

Both are telling the truth, describing pretty much exactly what happened. The conflict lies in how each of them punctuates it.

When we punctuate an interaction, we choose a beginning point and an endpoint that support our interpretation of what happened. Judy frames this argument as having started days earlier when she began asking Ken to pay the bill. Ken says it started when Judy laid into him. When she shoots that argument down, he suggests a second starting point: when he asked if there was enough money in the account.

Their different punctuation choices chopped the sequence of events into conflicting segments, distracting them from the bigger picture—that they've moved from addressing the issue to attacking each other's perspective on the issue.

If they can appreciate the role punctuation plays, they might be able to step back and see the sequence of events as a whole.

CONSIDER THIS . . .

Your willingness to alter how you punctuate an exchange reveals your capacity to be flexible.

Four Ways to Stop Conflict in Its Tracks

If you've ever played a musical instrument, you know what it's like to practice a piece, make a mistake, stop and start over, only to make the same mistake again. The spot where your playing went wrong can acquire an energy that's difficult to overcome. Each time you approach it, you anticipate the mistake, making it more likely to occur.

Because relationships operate in patterns and cycles, they can have sticking places too. These can be incredibly frustrating. For example, every time Aiden and Tim discuss how they manage money, Tim brings up Aiden's failed attempt at day trading on the stock market. In frustration, Aiden wonders out loud when Tim will "let go of the past." And Tim wonders if Aiden has really "learned his lesson."

Since the definition of being stuck is doing the same thing over and over with no change, the key to getting unstuck is doing something different or new.

Here are four things you can do when you find yourself in that familiar, frustrating stuck spot in your relationship. Each one offers an opportunity to take a fresh perspective. From this new point of view you are more likely to see a new direction forward.

Take a revolutionary pause. Rather than focusing on the specifics of the sticking point, take a revolutionary pause. The revolutionary pause is more than stepping back from the situation and counting to ten. It's active and intentional. As Viktor Frankl pointed out, between stimulus and response there is a space where you have the power to choose your response.

Claim that space and use it to take in the big picture of what's happening. From there it's easier to recognize: "Oh, this is just a particular spot in our relationship. It isn't the whole relationship." Noticing that it's only a small part of your relationship lets you consider it from a different, more productive view.

Shake it off. Interestingly, how you are in your relationship is largely physical. Tension shows up clearly in the body, and getting stuck usually brings on tension. There is also a lot of evidence that trauma of any variety is stored in the body.

If you have ever seen footage of a gazelle who is chased by a cheetah and escapes its predator, you may have seen it do an interesting thing. As soon as it knows it's safe, it does a massive body shrug. It literally shakes off the trauma its body is holding from barely escaping death.

The next time you find yourself in a serious standoff with your partner, consider taking a moment to retreat to a private space and shake it off. From head to toe, move your body as if you were shrugging off something unwanted.

Cultivate curiosity. In day-to-day relating, couples can experience many "snags." Snags make us take a second glance at something. They prompt thoughts like "What did he mean by that?" or "I can't remember the last time we really laughed together."

Sometimes a snag will turn into paralysis. Introducing curiosity can loosen things up remarkably. Ask yourself

 questions like "What am I really trying to accomplish?" "What I'm doing that makes my partner so defensive?" or "Who does my partner remind me of when we get to this stuck place?"

Questioning yourself in an open and curious way can lead to a different stance, which, in turn, can lead to a different outcome.

Pay attention to the choreography of the moment. People get stuck not just in emotional or intellectual patterns. They also get stuck in patterns of space and time. Instead of doing what you usually do—perhaps standing your ground or closing in for the "kill"—consider doing something different, such as moving toward your partner with openness and acceptance.

If taking a "time out" and leaving the scene is what you always do, think about not leaving. Instead take on an open posture. Make eye contact in a softer way. Pay attention to how your facial expression and even how you are holding your hands might be contributing to the impasse.

CONSIDER THIS . . .

If you have only one way to manage conflict,
you aren't managing it very well.

There Are No
Drama-Free Relationships

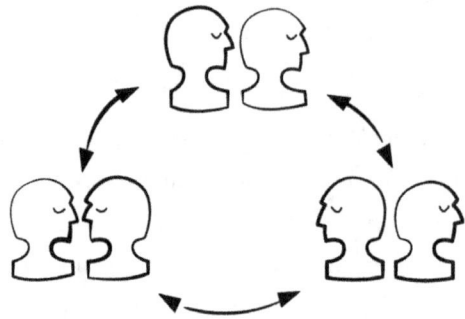

Humans are creatures of habit. Our behavior easily falls into predictable patterns that we repeat over and over. It's not so much that
we want to do this. The pattern just becomes so ingrained that we
repeat it without thinking.

For example, there's a one-lane bridge I must cross on my
way home from the office. The other day it was closed for repairs.
Several days earlier I'd seen the notice that the bridge would be
closed. Even so, that evening I took the same old route and then had
to backtrack and find an alternate way home.

Partnership is often like this. We do something that in
retrospect we realize wasn't the best. This isn't out of malice. We do
it without thinking. It's habitual.

The Drama Triangle, a model of human interaction first
developed in the 1960s by psychiatrist Stephen Karpman,
offers a view into habitual patterns in relationships. The model

identifies three possible roles we can assume—victim, rescuer, and persecutor—and suggests that these roles shape the dynamic of every interaction between people.

The roles are interdependent: A victim needs both a persecutor and a rescuer. A rescuer needs both a victim and a persecutor. And a persecutor needs both a victim and a rescuer.

For example, a parent who sets limits on a child's behavior is experienced as a persecutor by the child, who feels like a victim, and the child may then look to the other parent as a rescuer. Or a customer feels like a victim in an altercation with a customer service representative, who appears to the customer as a persecutor. The supervisor could then swoop in and be the rescuer of either the customer or the customer service representative.

These roles are a normal part of relationship dynamics, and each role is functional depending on the circumstances. Problems arise, however, when we take up residence in one role and consistently avoid the others—a victim, for instance, who can't see him- or herself as anything other than a victim may go to great lengths to maintain a sense of victimhood. This commitment to the role limits the ability to see oneself and the situation from different perspectives and therefore limits problem resolution and interpersonal growth.

Though the roles exist in casual interaction, they are much more pronounced in conflict. If you find yourself in constant conflict with your partner, pay attention to your interactions from the point of view of the Drama Triangle. Notice whether you gravitate toward one role more than the other two. If you do, then remind yourself that the other roles are available to you as well. The point is to avoid being stuck in one of them.

You want to find ways of productively moving around the triangle so that you're not stuck repeating the persistent, undesirable behavior that comes with being entrenched in a particular role.

CONSIDER THIS . . .

Drama is engaging. Being dramatic in different ways is engaging and productive.

Could You Be a Persecutor?

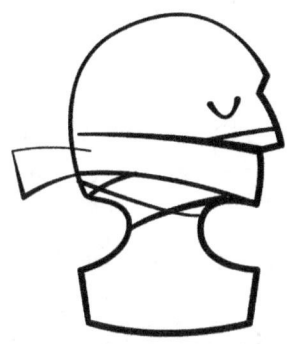

There is a notion out there that if you can't inflict pain, you can't be in an intimate relationship. That sounds harsh, for sure. But it's true.

Occasionally, one partner needs to become a persecutor for the relationship to move forward. If you take on the persecutor role with this intention, pay close attention to your motivation. Are you just venting anger? Or are you compassionately pointing out something that needs to change?

Persecution in its most mild forms can actually be healthy. If you are being yourself fully in your partner's company, there will be times, even in the most benign circumstances, when this is painful to your partner. People who always make sure their partner is comfortable at the cost of their own desires are denying themselves the experience of fully existing. Here's how this goes.

A healthy relationship requires two psychologically and emotionally whole individuals. Since human beings are as unique as snowflakes, these two whole individuals are, by definition, different from each other. And when two different people encounter each other, the potential for conflict is present.

For example,

Jason, who loves his husband, Tom, likes to watch light, happy TV. He likes sitcoms. He even enjoys shows that have a laugh track.

Tom, on the other hand, doesn't like sitcoms, particularly ones with a laugh track. He thinks, "How funny can something really be if you're told when to laugh?" Tom likes British crime dramas. They are dense, character focused, and often dark. He likes the grit-and-grime realism of those shows.

When Jason asks Tom to sit down with him and watch a sitcom, he is being himself in Tom's company. In so doing, he is inflicting something unpleasant on Tom. You could say he is, in some small way, the persecutor. And you would be right!

Now, is this a big deal? No, it isn't. In terms of the roles of the Drama Triangle, it's important for Jason to occasionally play the persecutor role, "persecuting" Tom in ways that aren't genuinely hurtful. If he declines to be himself (if he watches only British crime shows with Tom and never asks him to watch sitcoms with him), he would be leaving his true self outside the relationship. He would be accommodating Tom while diminishing the separateness necessary for a meaningful intimate relationship.

CONSIDER THIS . . .
To always avoid hurting your partner
is to avoid meaningful change.

Could You Be a Victim?

Life isn't fair!

That's hardly news. By the time you've passed your second birthday, you have probably experienced life's unfairness, even if you don't yet understand it. It's tough to come away from such experiences without feeling like a victim.

The Drama Triangle helps us see that while being a victim in a certain context is perfectly legitimate and likely true, identifying with that role in most contexts is dysfunctional. Said differently: Being a victim is an event; it has a beginning and an end. To identify with the victim role is to make victimhood a lifestyle.

The way out of victimhood is to access one of the other roles.

For instance, when someone who has been hurt sets out to help others who have been similarly hurt, he or she is shifting from victim to rescuer. This can be a step toward regaining power by feeling good about oneself and perhaps even about the pain one has experienced. When that person sets out to right the wrong by filing a lawsuit or making a public accusation, he or she is shifting from victim to persecutor. This too is a way of regaining power.

When your partner says, "I don't understand why you have to bring up politics when we are out with friends. It makes me uncomfortable," it's easy to feel like a victim. What comes next? You could identify further with the role of victim and feel sorry for yourself. (Truth be told, there's something kind of wonderful about feeling sorry for yourself.) Or you could shift to the role of rescuer and make your partner's life better by changing your behavior. Or you could shift to the persecutor role, standing up for yourself and insisting that it's perfectly legitimate to bring up current events.

Here's the takeaway.

Acknowledge when you are a victim. From there, move toward one of the other roles. By moving away from the victim role, you add options to the situation and even to your life. You give yourself and those around you a chance to see you as someone who's flexible and relatable rather than insistent on a particular point of view.

CONSIDER THIS . . .

To acknowledge victimhood is to acknowledge weakness. To acknowledge weakness is to identify a starting place for intimacy.

Could You Be a Rescuer?

We live in a world where things are often divided into black and white—good guys and bad guys. Most people want to be good guys. And even when you want to be bad, it's often because you think that by being bad you can do good. Like Robin Hood, who stole from the rich to give to the poor. Or the "bad" cop who gets rid of the bad guys.

There's a lot of virtue in the rescue stance. When you rescue, you feel good about yourself, and those you rescue often love you for it. You might tend to rescue without giving it much thought. You notice what needs to be done and do it before your partner even thinks of it.

But there are downsides to rescuing. For one, you can develop an inflated view of your skills and power. You might begin to think there is no one and no situation you can't rescue.

For another, by rescuing someone you may prevent that person from learning a difficult lesson they are meant to learn. When your rescuing keeps someone from growing, it isn't something to feel good about.

Here's the takeaway:

Rescue but be careful. There may be unintended consequences.

CONSIDER THIS . . .

Being a rescuer can have unplanned repercussions.

A Paradox:
Sometimes Sacrifice
Is Better than Compromise

Navigating differences is a primary task a couple must do. The better they are able to do it, the more satisfying they find their relationship, while failing at it leads to tension, conflict, and dissatisfaction. It's as simple as that.

Compromise is a common approach to navigating differences: "Let's meet in the middle." And it works. For example, a couple agrees: "This Christmas we will spend with your family and next Christmas with mine." Or "You'd like to have sex three times a week and I'm more comfortable with once a week, so we'll compromise at sex twice a week."

Compromises like these make for a smooth-running relationship. They demonstrate an unmistakable level of care and love for each other. But what about those times when the differences aren't easily resolved?

A simple example is being a morning person versus a night person. Though being a morning person or a night person seems hardwired, with sufficient discipline and will power those natural tendencies can be changed. But not easily. For a night person to get up early to have coffee and chat with a morning person is a sacrifice more than a compromise.

Differences in values can be even harder to navigate.

Consider Rich and Danielle, who love each other deeply and are committed to their partnership. Danielle wants to have another child. From childhood she longed for a large family. It was a part of their conversations before getting married, and she thought they were on the same page. Rich, on the other hand, wants to limit their family to two children. He grew up in an unstable family situation and, despite their conversations years ago, has become determined to keep the family small. He wants to be sure he can meet the financial and time demands of having a wife and children.

Rich and Danielle each feel betrayed by the other, essentially taking the stance: "If you loved me the way you say you do, you'd see how important this is to me, and you'd give me what I want."

Deeply held desires and values like these are often profoundly attached to a person's definition of a good life, and the thought of letting them go usually brings up intense emotions. At best, letting go of a deeply held belief in favor of a competing belief creates anxiety. At worst, it's terrifying. Fear eliminates constructive compromise as an option. How do you compromise something so deeply woven into the fabric of your life?

When a couple faces this kind of impasse, it seems to me that love calls for both to notice their fears, perhaps question those fears, and be open to sacrifice. This requires a lot of courage and discernment.

Unhealthy sacrifice is born of martyrdom, while healthy sacrifice is unilateral and unconditional. A healthy sacrifice is a gift given without expectation of anything in return. In this case, Rich might say,

"I will give you the opportunity to have a larger family and rethink my need for security and stability."

Or Danielle might say,

"I give up my desire for a larger family in favor of your need for security."

Most of us are inclined to notice what we are getting out of a relationship. When times are tough, we might entertain compromise as a way of getting at least some of what we want. The prospect of getting none of what we want while our partner gets all of what he or she wants can feel unfair.

Paradoxically, embracing the unfairness of sacrifice has the potential to deepen self and the relationship in ways compromise simply can't. While compromise can foster closeness, sacrifice, offered freely and accepted humbly, can create intimacy.

Sacrifice invites looking deeply into the nature of love and drawing out the purest and most valuable aspects of that love. Compromise contributes to stability. Sacrifice, done well, generates growth.

CONSIDER THIS . . .

Your willingness to sacrifice speaks volumes about your ability to sustain a long-term relationship.

Is Change Even Possible?

What to Do When You Want Something Better

What Comes Naturally

Imagine for a moment that you are afraid of spiders. (If you are actually afraid of spiders, this will be easy.) You walk into the kitchen to fill your water glass. As you approach the sink, you see a spider crouched in the corner, its legs and body dark against the white porcelain. You recoil, gasp, and step back across the room.

This is an example of doing what comes naturally. Quite likely, no one taught you to respond to spiders that way. It's a completely automatic response.

Most often, people's behavior is a natural response to their experience. For example, your natural response to anger might be to become angry yourself. Or it might be to withdraw and disengage.

In a relationship, natural responses, repeated over time, create patterns of exchange between partners. A pattern of exchange can be around a specific issue such as money or around a simple daily interaction like how the couple greets each other in the morning.

Improving your relationship often requires changing an established pattern, which requires that one or both of you stop doing what comes naturally and start doing things that feel unnatural.

This can be difficult. Because a peaceful, contented life requires a certain predictability, we are often reluctant to disrupt an established pattern, even if the disruption might lead to a better quality of relationship. It's the old story of preferring the devil you know over the devil you don't know.

While introducing something new into the relationship comes about more easily if embraced by both parties, this isn't essential. With enough imagination, courage, patience, and persistence one partner can often change the course of a relationship without the active participation of the other.

For example, instead of responding to your partner's anger with your own anger or by withdrawing, you can choose to respond with openness and willingness to dialogue. Your new response will feel unnatural. You will hope that your partner responds well, acknowledging your unexpected response by making a dialogue shift him/herself.

Because he or she might not respond as you hope, doing what feels unnatural comes with some risk. However, taking that risk increases the chances of making a significant and desirable change in your relationship.

CONSIDER THIS . . .

If you only do what comes naturally,
nothing will change.

First-Order Versus
Second-Order Change

Whether in the aftermath of trauma or out of garden-variety boredom, most couples at some point start saying, tacitly or overtly, that something different needs to happen in their relationship. They start looking for something fresh, something alive—a new pattern of relating.

It's relatively easy to modify the form of an existing pattern. If a couple usually spends Friday evenings together, it doesn't take much to add going out to their Friday plans. If they typically make love four times a month, it isn't difficult to add or subtract one occasion.

These are examples of first-order change. They are changes in frequency, duration, or intensity.

Challenges arise when a couple wants to not just modify but break an existing pattern and replace it with a new pattern. One partner might say, "I want us to be together differently. I don't just want us to be able to talk about something difficult; I want us to talk about it in a new way. I want our conversations to feel fresh, spontaneous, and inviting."

This is a request for a second-order change. It's a desire for something new and therefore quite unfamiliar yet desirable for the promise it offers.

Genuinely new behaviors are rarely done well the first few times they are attempted. As an example, most of us have a post-shower drying-off routine that we repeat daily and unconsciously. The next time you shower, start drying yourself at a different place on your body and see how it goes. You will probably feel clumsy, perhaps confused or even frustrated.

Similarly, when a second-order change is introduced into a relationship, a certain amount of clumsiness and confusion may arise. Failure may happen, even repeated failure. Occasionally the frustration can get intense enough to cause the couple to throw up their hands and revert to the old, familiar way of interacting.

Anne-Laure le Cunff, in her book *Tiny Experiments,* suggests an experimental approach as a way to experience a new pattern while minimizing the risk that change implies. The upside of experimentation is that even a failed experiment offers valuable information about how to design the next experiment.

Here's an example.

Rick and Melanie have been married for twenty years. Both are quick to affirm their love for each other, and both acknowledge that their intimate life has been flat for years. They have "maintenance sex" once or twice a month. Yet both say they want more passion. They want to imagine each other differently. They want to look at their own and each other's body through different eyes. They want to make love as opposed to simply having sex. They are looking for a second-order change.

To engage a second-order change in how they approach sex, Rick and Melanie agree to create a small experiment. They decide to start expressing sexual desire on Tuesday with love notes, tender eye contact, kisses, and hugs. After continuing this for three days, on Friday they will make love. Further, they agree to engage in this experiment twice a month for the next three months, after which they will have a conversation about its impact on their sex life.

When the goal is to create a second-order change, the outcome can't be guaranteed. By implementing their experiment Rick and Melanie embrace that uncertainty actively and deliberately. The experiment sets the stage for a tiny shift that has the potential to create radical improvement in the way they relate to each other sexually.

CONSIDER THIS . . .

If you know something in your relationship needs to change but you don't know what that something is, you are looking for a second-order change.

It's Okay to Try to Change Your Partner

Couples in a committed relationship are generally advised

Don't try to change your partner. Accept them as they are.

Truth be told, this advice is useless because it asks people to do the impossible. Most couples spend months, if not years, trying to change each other.

Everyone wants their partner to be better. Everyone wants improved communication, more and better affection, better money management, a better parenting style, and much more. All of these areas of living and of partnership deserve attention and improvement. So, couples are better advised: "Go ahead and do your best to change your partner for the better."

It's not a matter of whether to try to change your partner, because you inevitably will. What matters is the method.

If you do it lovingly, with respect, empathy, and patience, your partner will likely experience your efforts as supportive.

If you do it out of exasperation, impatience, and condescension, your partner is sure to resist.

The next time you try to change your partner, notice how much love and respect are in your approach. Chances are, if you get pushback, it's because you've let frustration be the dominant emotion as you try to create positive change.

CONSIDER THIS . . .

Helping your partner change
is a way of loving him/her.

Why "Stupid" Topics
Create Heated Arguments

While there are many ways of viewing how relationships work, the existentialist perspective is especially useful for its emphasis on meaning. It assumes that both people in a partnership are driven to find meaning and that the choices they make help create that meaning.

Because choices can only be made in the here and now, the present moment is precious. And none of us has an infinite number of present moments available. While circumstances sometimes make this fact painfully palpable, most of the time awareness of life's eventual end hums in the back of our mind like the sound of traffic outside. We know it's there, but we live as if it weren't.

In *The Denial of Death*, author Ernest Becker points out that awareness of our eventual demise is innate to us. We are always unconsciously watching the "play clock" of our lives as it ticks down, measuring the meaning of our actions against death, whether our ultimate demise or the demise of a certain characteristic or stance.

If you and your partner are fighting and you are trying to understand why, stop wondering about the topic of the conflict. Rather, wonder if the fighting is rooted in an existential fear of death—in this case, the death of a particular way of finding meaning.

That may sound a little crazy, but notice how hard a couple will fight over some little issue. Evidently, for them it's not a little issue at all. The argument is, in some way, a life-and-death struggle.

This is sometimes revealed in the language they use. A surprising number of people in long-term committed relationships eventually say to themselves, "If I stay with him/her another day [or week or month or year], it will be the death of me." They may think—or even say—things like "I can't take this anymore!" or "You're killing me."

Symbolically, it could be true.

Most people can accept the occasional challenge to how they create meaning in life. It's when the occasional challenge turns into a pattern that it begins to feel "lethal."

CONSIDER THIS . . .

To embrace the importance of meaning is to lighten the burden of unhappiness.

Going in Circles Doesn't Mean There's No Progress

Almost every couple at some point says "It seems like we're going in circles. We're not making any progress. We go over the same things again and again."

Though circularity can be discouraging, it doesn't have to be.

There is more than one way of going around in a circle. The kind of circling a top does is essentially pointless. It may move from one spot to the next, but its movement isn't purposeful. The kind of circling a screw does as it is driven into a hole is different. Each time the screw turns a full circle it is moving in the desired direction.

If your relationship seems to be going in circles, remind yourself that this doesn't necessarily mean progress isn't being made. Look for subtle ways things might be changing. Is your attitude toward the problem you're addressing a bit different? Are there slight shifts in how you feel about your partner or yourself?

There's a lot of circularity in life. Seasons come and go in cycles—it's not like once we are done with winter, we never have winter again. If we look closely, we can notice progressive change: this winter the bare branches of the young maple in the front yard reach a foot higher than they did a year ago.

If a couple can embrace circularity as part of change, they are more likely to notice the subtle changes occurring each time an issue shows up.

CONSIDER THIS . . .

Going in circles can be both enlightening and comforting.

Is It a
Spiritual Problem?

Thanks to the likes of Dr. Phil and TV shows such as *In Treatment*, *Shrinking*, and even *The Sopranos*, we live in a "therapy-wise" culture. Any stigma associated with seeing a therapist is long gone. Few people blink an eye at the idea of an active unconscious. And although many are uncomfortable with the power of emotions, most people recognize their importance.

Even so, clients sometimes report that therapy isn't producing the changes they desire. They tell me they've gained insight. They know what to do and why. But the insights and skills they've gained haven't resolved their issues.

My response is to ask:

"Is it possible that you are stuck because you're not recognizing the spiritual dimension of the problem?"

I'm not wondering about my clients' relationship with God or a higher power. I'm asking about their relationship with the traditional virtues and vices such as courage and fear, humility and pride, generosity and greed.

You can know exactly what to say, when to say it, and why saying it is necessary. But if you don't have the courage to say it, those insights are useless.

You can know the how, when, and why of forgiving someone. But if you don't have the humility necessary to be authentic, the rest is empty effort.

No amount of insight, skill, or, for that matter, medication will bring about the change you seek unless you bring to it the spirit of something larger than yourself—something like courage, humility, generosity, patience, love, hope.

CONSIDER THIS . . .

Sometimes the most important factors leading to relationship satisfaction are intangible.

Are You Stuck or Have You Just Parked?

From time to time, a couple can feel like their relationship has come to a grinding halt. Frustrations escalate, tempers flare, and life feels unbearable.

It's easy to label this experience as "being stuck." But it could be something else.

Stuck is when you can't move forward. Your car is on ice—wheels spin, there's no traction. A relationship is stuck when both partners genuinely want a solution and they've tried everything they know to try but can't create movement.

Couples often think they are stuck when they really aren't. Instead, one or both are parked.

Being parked and being stuck share some features, the most obvious being the absence of movement. Another shared feature is the presence of frustration. Whether a couple is stuck or parked, they usually feel exasperated and annoyed.

Here is the difference: When you are stuck, you *can't* move forward. When you are parked, you *won't* move forward.

People often won't move forward because, for a variety of quite logical reasons, they are afraid to take the next step. So, they put themselves in park and label what's happening as "stuck."

The car on ice is stuck because of conditions outside itself—the surface is slick. So also, people tend to attribute their circumstance to factors outside their control, often out of fear. You feel stuck because your partner won't listen to you. You feel stuck because your boss won't give you a raise. You can't move because someone won't do what you need them to do.

If you're feeling stuck in your relationship, look at the situation closely. Look at yourself closely. Notice whether you are frightened. Ask yourself if fear has led you to park your life.

The good news about discovering that you're not stuck, you've simply parked your life, is that you have the power to unpark it. As it is with the driver of the car on the roadside, the controls are in your hands.

It might be that you are genuinely stuck. That certainly happens. But it might also be that you've chosen to put yourself in park because the route forward you've identified is just too scary. Once you've acknowledged and addressed your fear, the possibility of movement becomes more likely.

CONSIDER THIS . . .

Putting yourself in "park" is prioritizing safety over growth.

A Paradox:
Accept Your Partner
to Change Your Partner

Most people, at some point, are caught between wanting to accept their partner fully—the enlightened awareness we read about in books on relationship—and having to put up with some almost intolerable relationship circumstance.

> "You mean I am supposed to accept the fact that he keeps lying to me about smoking? I hate it! I can't stand the smell, not to mention all the money he throws away on cigarettes every week."

Or...

> "I've done my best to accept her way of parenting. But come on! Is there no end to the coddling? When will she put some limits on unacceptable behavior?"

If you accept your partner fully as he or she is at the expense of honoring your own wants, needs, and even values, you are out of integrity with yourself. If you are certain your partner must change and insist on it, you can feel like a tyrant—selfish and callous.

In this situation, acceptance may be the best route to change. You can try changing your partner's behavior by dispensing rewards and punishments, nagging, threatening, or cajoling. But the truth is, only after your partner feels completely accepted by you will he or she consider letting down his or her defenses. And only after those defenses are set aside is your partner likely to consider seriously the change you want him or her to make.

Acceptance is often expressed as validation. If you want your partner to feel accepted, you must validate him or her, as well as his or her actions. For example, "Given what I know about how you grew up, I understand how you'd want to be soft and accommodating with the children." This is acceptance. This is not agreement.

Through validation and acceptance, you create a safe space where your partner is more likely to set aside resistance and become open to conversation and eventual change.

CONSIDER THIS . . .

Nothing of consequence changes
until it is fully accepted.

What Brings
Us Together?

Cultivating an Intimate Connection

Falling in Love

Most people have a soft spot for falling in love. They treasure the moment they were first drawn to someone who could meet their emotional needs and whose needs they could readily meet in exchange. They long to reexperience the intensity, drive, and passion that came with it. Those who haven't yet fallen in love usually anticipate the experience with eagerness. They may envy those who have already had their shot and puzzle over those who pass it off as unimportant.

Having watched hundreds of couples fall in love and live out the effects of that experience, sometimes over decades, I've concluded there are two perspectives on it.

One is that falling in love represents a kind of divine madness. To commit to spending the rest of your life with someone demands that you be out of your mind and falling in love is nature's way of generating the hysteria necessary to take such an audacious leap.

The other view is that falling in love is a rare moment of complete clarity. When you fall in love, you feel wholly seen for who you are and believe you fully see your partner for who he or she is. Rather than clouding your vision, falling in love clarifies and validates. Out of this absolute clarity—absolute sanity—the decision to commit becomes reasonable.

Which way you choose to understand this powerful experience says a lot about how you might regard it over time. If you view falling in love as temporary insanity, you may devalue it and its product: commitment to a lifelong union. If you see it as a moment of genuinely seeing and being seen, you are more likely to cherish it and the relationship it fosters.

CONSIDER THIS . . .

Love always invites us to move
into uncharted territory.

Two Fears That Accompany Falling in Love

It is said that fear and love cannot coexist—that fear makes real love impossible and real love eliminates fear. In an ideal world and for those who are enlightened, I'm sure this is true. But most of us don't live in an ideal world, and few of us are genuinely enlightened. In fact, the struggle between fear and love occurs daily for most people. They just don't recognize it for what it is.

Fear in the context of an intimate relationship takes one of two forms: fear of abandonment or fear of engulfment.

Those who fear abandonment (often unconsciously) expect that their partner will eventually leave. Even when the relationship is relatively stable, there's a nagging sense that sooner or later their loved one will walk out the door and never come back. That sense is enhanced with thoughts like "I'm sure he's getting tired of me," "I just don't have what she really wants," "When he discovers who

I really am, he'll call it quits." If the fear of abandonment is strong enough, it can become self-fulfilling. It can push the other partner into questioning the relationship.

Those who fear engulfment (often unconsciously) expect that their partner is going to limit their freedom. When their partner expresses a normal desire for more affection or more information, they feel smothered. To claim the space they need to feel free and safe, they may withdraw, or they may attack. If the fear of engulfment is strong enough, it can lead to deception. Rather than being open and straightforward about what's going on, the frightened person may offer vague responses or resort to lying.

Whether you are inclined toward fear of abandonment or fear of engulfment, the first step is to admit the fear to yourself. This can take some self-reflection and courage. Once you have recognized and named the fear, ground yourself as much as possible in the love that transcends momentary anxiety. This can be done by recalling your early experience of falling in love or by identifying the virtues that often accompany love such as patience and acceptance. Recognize that neither abandonment nor engulfment has the power to extinguish a genuine and deeply rooted love.

CONSIDER THIS . . .
Empowerment often lies in moving
toward what frightens you.

Dancing with Your Lover's Daemon

You can do all kinds of things to make your relationship better. You can improve how you communicate. You can increase your patience and compassion. But you still have to deal with the instinctual way you respond to life events. It can be softened, even subdued, but it can't be eliminated. This bit of hardwiring is called temperament by some. Others regard it as a habit of mind. I like to call it a person's daemon.

Just as it behooves you to learn to dance with your own daemon *(see the essay on page 59)*, growing a successful committed relationship calls for also learning to dance with your partner's daemon.

When your daemon and your lover's daemon meet, things sometimes go amazingly well. Your temperaments may dance with each other so compatibly that being together feels effortless. This happens, for example, when one partner's need to be helpful meets the other's need to be helped.

At other times, the two daemons' meeting feels more like mortal combat—for instance, when the helpful partner's version of helping doesn't match the other partner's definition of help.

Janice and Ted have learned that to maintain a healthy committed relationship, they need to be on a first-name basis with their own daemon and the other's, greeting them with respect and interest, not judgment, when they show up. Here's Janice's telling of one of their interactions:

> Just the other day, Ted and I got caught in a daemon struggle—his constant desire for more entangling with my chronic caution. They often collide around time, attention, and affection, and I'd started talking about an event in my past that didn't include him. He felt the pain of not having me fully in that moment, while I wasn't ready to let go of the memory and be fully present with him.
>
> In an instant we felt our daemons flare, posture, and prepare to fight. His jumped right in, rattling off several times when I'd withheld myself from him. Mine came right back, naming occasions when his desires were unreasonable. We were off to the races. A few hours later, after some serious wound licking, we reconciled.

If Janice could experience Ted's desire for more as a genuine impulse to improve their relationship, they would get along great. When she sees it as demanding or controlling, things don't go so well. Ted would do well to regard Janice's caution as an authentic effort to keep them safe by slowing things down. Things go badly when he sees it as stubbornness.

Acknowledging your daemon and your partner's reveals points in your relationship where growth is possible, even if it is difficult. When your daemons dance, they uncover differences that beg to be acknowledged, respected, and accepted.

CONSIDER THIS . . .

Working with your partner's daemon
is an act of love.

When Sexual Desire and Performance Meet

For the most part, sexual performance is straightforward. While there are variations on the theme, performance itself is relatively uncomplicated.

Human sexual desire, on the other hand, is complicated and nuanced. It can be powerful and relentless at one moment and fragile and elusive at the next. The complexity of desire is what makes sex such a remarkable route to intimate connection. But when the complexity of desire meets the straightforwardness of performance, confusion can follow.

A person may desire a sexual experience but not be able to perform—or be able to perform but not experience much in the way of desire. In each circumstance both the person and his or her partner are likely to feel that something is missing.

Desire at its best is personal and emotional.

It's what makes a sexual encounter meaningful, even healing. More than being able to perform and respond sexually, most of us want to experience desire and being desired. We want to be wanted.

In a good sexual encounter, the internal experience of desire and the external, physical expression of that desire as sexual performance coincide. Typically, this involves a back and forth between the body's ability to transmit and respond to physical stimulation and how we feel with and about our partner.

While desire can be strong in a casual encounter, it tends to be superficial and fleeting, not the kind of desire that inspires connection and growth. A committed relationship provides the best environment for in-depth exploration of sexual desire and physical expression of that desire. Because there is no need for repeated getting-to-know-you exchanges, a couple can start an encounter from a deeper place and achieve a more profound experience of intimacy.

CONSIDER THIS . . .
Sexual familiarity precedes sexual growth.

Sexual Accelerators and Sexual Brakes

The Dual Control Model of sexual response, developed in the late 1990s at the Kinsey Institute, suggests that each of us has a set of triggers that move us toward sexual expression (accelerators) and another set of triggers that move us away from it (brakes).

The stereotype is that women have more brake triggers and men have more accelerator triggers, but I haven't observed that with the couples I see. In fact, when a couple stops having sex, the man is more often the one who has put on the brakes. While this can be for a variety of reasons, the most prevalent is fear of performance failure. Once a man experiences erectile dysfunction, anxiety sets in. He may start to avoid sexual encounters—to apply the brakes.

A person's tendency to press the accelerator or apply the brakes can also be the result of early sexual experiences, good or bad. Or it might be "hardwired"; for instance, someone who is temperamentally shy and reticent might exhibit more brakes than accelerator.

Regardless of their cause, it's vital to begin a sexual encounter by accepting our predilections and patterns, since acceptance creates an environment conducive to change and growth. It's equally vital to pay attention to the sexual context—to both partners' sexual past and to the physical and emotional features of the present setting—as this provides a framework for accepting and managing accelerators and brakes.

CONSIDER THIS . . .

Acceleration is more likely to happen once the brakes are acknowledged.

Set and Setting for a Good Sexual Experience

Like all good experiences, a good sexual experience depends on "set and setting"—the right mindset and the right physical and social environment. Devoting some time and thought to applying this wisdom can greatly improve your love life.

What constitutes a good sexual encounter is highly individual. When two people come together to make love, what satisfies both is all the more complex. Even so, some elements of a good sexual experience are widely common.

Mindset—how you think about the sexual experience you want to have—is primary for a good sexual encounter. Mindset as it relates to sex is about finding the right mix of desire and empathy. Desire is all about me, while empathy is all about my partner. If desire overshadows empathy, I may come across as demanding, at worst even abusive. If empathy overshadows desire, I may come across as tentative and lacking genuine interest.

Making this more complex: I want my partner to be aware of her desire because that's arousing to me. At the same time, I want my partner to be empathic and sensitive to me because that lets me know she cares about me as much as she cares about her own satisfaction.

Setting—a context conducive to the sexual experience you want—is a close second to mindset. If I know my partner responds favorably to a long, sensuous back rub done in a neat, clean, candlelit bedroom and I'm interested in having some good sex, why don't I clean the bedroom, light some candles, and give her the back rub? Is it because I'm lazy? . . . perhaps. Or I feel like she doesn't deserve it? . . . perhaps. Or there just isn't enough time? . . . perhaps. There can be all kinds of reasons.

Sometimes we simply need things to be clearly spelled out. So here's a before-sex checklist of questions to help you align your mindset and create the setting for a satisfying experience.

- How am I feeling physically?

- Has my partner said anything lately to indicate how he/she is feeling physically?

- What's my mood? What's his/hers?

- Do I trust him/her? Am I trustworthy?

- How are we with the question of who is in charge of our sexual relationship?

- Do I feel emotionally connected to him/her?

- Do I feel desired? Do I desire? And to what level?

- Do I like where we are going to have sex? Will he/she like it?

- Are we interested in experimenting with something new?

- Are we ready to be open with each other?

- How do we want to feel about this tomorrow?

Granted, most of us want sex to be more spontaneous than a checklist suggests. But as the saying goes, "If a thing is worth doing, it's worth doing well." That includes sex. A little thoughtful preparation may be just what your relationship needs.

CONSIDER THIS . . .

Connection occurs in the interplay between your and your partner's desires.

Emotion: Neither Too Much nor Too Little

Sarah has always "worn her feelings on her sleeve." Sometimes she's self-conscious about this tendency, but mostly she sees her easy access to her emotions as an asset. As a child she could slip almost seamlessly from a temper tantrum to "playing mom" with her dolls. The flow of emotions from anger and disappointment to love and caring comes naturally to her.

Greg, on the other hand, grew up in a family that didn't say a whole lot, certainly not about how they felt. In fact, emotions didn't really matter. What mattered was getting stuff done. Of course, he feels his emotions keenly when his favorite football team is in a close and important game or when a driver cuts him off in traffic. But mostly he sees his emotions as an annoyance that clouds his thinking.

When Greg and Sarah got together, each saw the other's orientation around the expression of emotion as a strength. Greg found Sarah's easy access to her feelings refreshing, even exciting. Sarah found Greg's cool-headedness steady and reassuring. She felt safe around him.

After a year of partnership, however, Sarah began feeling a little lonely. Greg didn't seem to understand what she was going through. Greg, meanwhile, was confused by Sarah's unhappiness. He was doing all he could to make life good for them. He stayed on top of tasks around the house and was ready to help when she needed something done.

When they tried to talk things out, each one felt like the other was speaking a foreign language. So, they did what people often do when they don't feel understood— each pressed his or her point of view, as if simply saying it louder would get it across. Which of course got them nowhere.

To go forward, Greg and Sarah would do well to, first, acknowledge that emotions are central to human interactions, and, second, accept each other's perspective on emotions.

If Greg embraces Sarah's expression of emotion as her genuine effort to participate fully in their relationship, she will likely feel validated and, therefore, not need to express them so vehemently. By the same token, if Sarah validates Greg's quiet strength as its own expression of emotion (e.g., confidence) he will likely begin to see the value in more overt expression of what he's feeling. *(For more on how acceptance can produce change, see page 121.)*

Emotions need to be respected. They make us feel alive. They connect us to each other. They give a relationship texture and provide the raw material for a meaningful bond between partners.

CONSIDER THIS . . .

Nothing in an intimate relationship is free of emotion.

Relating to Your Emotions

Most of us think about (even obsess over) our relationship with our body—a lot. We look in the mirror, turning this way and that, to assess how we feel about the body we inhabit. Indeed, whole ad campaigns have been launched encouraging people (usually girls) to cultivate a positive relationship with their body as a step toward developing a positive attitude toward themselves.

Generally speaking, we spend much less time and energy wondering about our relationship with our emotions. Perhaps that's because parents and peers encouraged us to minimize or deny our emotions while growing up.

"I'm sorry you feel bad. Give it a few days and you will feel better."

"That's tough but think about how much worse other people have it."

In fact, if you have a poor relationship with your emotions, there's a good chance you'll have a poor relationship with the person you've chosen as a partner. An emotionally rich and rewarding partnership calls for both people to have a healthy relationship with their emotions—to know what they are feeling and to feel comfortable sharing it.

Consider this exchange:

Beth: "How are you feeling about what happened at work today?"

Dan: "I don't know. Not feeling much of anything about it."

And this exchange:

Beth: "How are you feeling about what happened at work today?"

Dan: "I've tried to get a handle on it. Mostly I feel disappointed. Beyond that, it's confusing and really annoying."

In the first example, Dan's relationship with his emotions is almost nonexistent. Consequently, Beth knows very little about how Dan experienced his workday. In the second, he demonstrates a well-functioning relationship with his emotions by unapologetically identifying and expressing them. This allows Beth to know not only what he did at work but also how he feels about what he did. This added dimension is likely to increase their experience of being connected.

CONSIDER THIS . . .

How you relate to your emotions can determine the emotional climate of your relationship.

Improving How You Relate to Your Emotions

A central feature of Cognitive Behavioral Therapy (CBT), a building block of many forms of psychotherapy, is the cognitive triangle, which presents thoughts, actions, and emotions as equivalent elements in an equilateral triangle representing mental and relational health. However, current culture prioritizes thought and action over emotion. (Ironically, even the term "cognitive behavioral" highlights only the thought and action points on CBT's own triangle.) This minimizes the very feature that draws us into an intimate relationship.

When we minimize our emotions, we undermine the heart of what connects us to our loved one. When, on the other hand, we nourish our relationship with our own emotions, we also nourish our relationship with our partner.

Here are some suggestions for improving how you relate to the emotional part of you. Each of them implies there is a "you" that's separate from your emotions (just as there is a "you" that's separate from your thoughts and actions).

Know that you are not your emotions. It's natural to experience your emotions as you. When you say, for instance, "I am sad," you are identifying with the sadness; there is no you aside from the sadness. But in fact, there is always a "you" who is experiencing the emotion. In other words, you have an emotion, it doesn't have you. Awareness of this distinction allows you to relate to your emotions and thus to make choices about how you express them.

Use the language of parts when referring to your emotions. Instead of "I am sad," try saying "There's a part of me that's sad." This shift leaves room for the truth that other aspects of you may simultaneously be feeling different emotions. For example, when an aging parent dies, a part of you is probably deeply sad, while another part is relieved that the inevitable has come and gone. By using the language of parts, you acknowledge the truth of what is going on for you without making it the whole truth.

Think of your emotions as signals or warning signs. When an emotion makes itself known, your job is to acknowledge it and determine what it is asking you to notice. In a way, a conversation between you and your emotion is taking place. For instance, when the smoke alarm goes off, it triggers an emotion . . . perhaps fear. The emotion then leads you to wonder whether the drapes are on fire or you've burned the toast. A "conversation" between the part of you that's afraid and the part of you that's assessing the situation will tell you whether you should call 911 or open a window and fan the smoke alarm until it turns off. Shutting down your emotions is like ignoring the smoke alarm, which is almost never a good idea.

Create a space for your emotional self. When an emotion shows up, imagine a space where you and the emotion are both present. Let that space be large enough for you to maintain an appropriate distance from the emotion so you can respond to it without being entangled with it. Finding the right distance from your emotions helps you develop a healthy relationship with them.

CONSIDER THIS . . .

To manage emotions, you first need to have a good relationship with them.

Developing an
Emotion Vocabulary

As infants we enter the world with a tiny repertoire of emotions: "I feel bad/uncomfortable/displeased" and "I feel good/comfortable/pleased." This simple dichotomy is adequate to get us through infancy, but it's not rich and varied enough to meet the needs of a developing human being.

As children grow, caregivers help them expand and deepen those two starter categories of emotion. When a child shows signs of distress, a parent might say, "You feel angry." The child then begins to assign the word "angry" to that emotional experience. This process continues through early childhood and into adulthood until we have a range of emotion words to accurately describe our experience.

If we are not taught a wide vocabulary for describing emotions, however, we can't productively communicate a range of emotions. This doesn't mean we don't feel and express a variety of emotions. It simply means we can't identify them and talk about them constructively.

A limited vocabulary of emotions leaves us in a real deficit in relationship, where conversations with our intimate partner often require complexity and nuance. It's a bit like an auto mechanic trying to fix a mechanical problem in a modern car without the necessary sophisticated tools.

Jason has just discovered that his wife, Megan, applied for a part-time job without discussing its impact on the family with him. The first words out of his mouth are "I am really upset that you didn't talk with me before doing this!"

There's no doubt that Jason is upset. Megan can see that in his stance, his face, his tone of voice. But what does he mean by "upset"? When a person's emotion vocabulary is limited, they often use vague labels like "upset." But what emotion is Jason actually feeling? Is he upset/confused? Upset/angry? Upset/resentful? Upset/feeling left out? The more specifically Jason can describe what he's feeling, the easier it will be for Megan to speak to that, and the more likely they are to have a productive conversation.

It is important to build a vocabulary of feeling words and experiment with using them. Try them on. See if they fit. Then see if your relationship improves because your newfound vocabulary helps your partner better understand what you are experiencing.

Here are a couple of ways to build your emotion vocabulary.

- Search the internet for "feeling words." You will find many lists. Go over them and find appropriate ways to use some of the new words you've found.

- When you watch a movie or series, put yourself in the shoes of one of the characters and ask yourself what you'd feel if you were in his/her circumstance.

CONSIDER THIS . . .
Where vocabulary is limited,
conversation is limited.

Intimacy and Closeness

"Closeness" and "intimacy" are often treated as synonyms—two words for the same thing. It's true that both are desirable goals in relationship. But they are actually two different experiences. Here's an example of each.

Greg and Roxanne have been together for almost 10 years. They've never regretted their decision to commit themselves to each other. In fact, they can't imagine not being together. When there's a project to do around the house, they do it together. If Greg is rolling the paint on the wall, Roxanne is painting the trim. They have the same definitions of "expensive" and "clean." They both go out of their way to avoid an argument. When differences between them show up, each dismisses the difference as unimportant. Arguments are so rare that they can't remember the last time they had one. They are very close.

Andrew and Monica met online and got married a year later. From their first coffee date, they felt the intense charge that often accompanies deep attraction. Their conversations are often long and sometimes heated. They don't always agree, but they always enjoy the depth of conviction each brings to their conversations. What they love most is the feeling of being accepted and respected by the other even when they disagree. Although they often notice the ways they are significantly different, neither of them ever feels judged. Their relationship is intimate.

One of these experiences is not better than the other. The best relationships include both closeness and intimacy.

If you're in a good relationship but feel that it has become cool, flat, even boring, you and your partner might be close but lack intimacy. If you love your partner but are overwhelmed by the intensity of your interactions, it's possible that you're intimate but lack the comfort and ease that comes with closeness.

A mostly close relationship can be heated up by identifying and engaging in reasonable risks. Taking risks together almost always enhances intimacy. Risk-taking can be as simple as trying a new restaurant with an unusual cuisine or as complicated as beginning couple therapy.

A mostly intimate relationship can be cooled down by identifying ways to appropriately increase the emotional space between you and your partner. Each of you having a personal interest or hobby that doesn't include yet is supported by the other is a great way to introduce more closeness. By supporting your partner's separate interest, you lovingly create both emotional and physical space. The space created moves the relationship away from the heat of intimacy and toward the cool comfort of closeness.

CONSIDER THIS . . .

A thriving relationship moves smoothly from intimacy to closeness and back again.

Why Is It So Hard to Stay in Step?

Maintaining an Intimate Connection

Zero-Sum and Non-Zero-Sum Relating

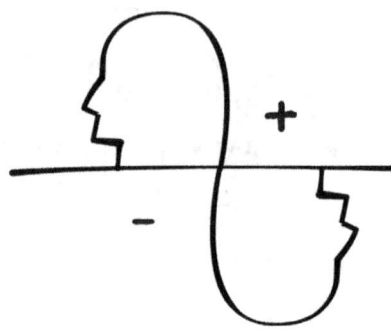

What might applied mathematics have to say about healthy, intimate relationships? Well, in terms of zero-sum game theory, it has quite a bit to say.

In a zero-sum situation, one person's gain means another person's loss. In a non-zero-sum situation, one person's gain does not necessarily mean the other person loses. It's even possible for both to gain.

Consider the difference between giving someone money and giving someone love. If I have ten dollars and give you five, I have only five left and you have an additional five. You gain and I lose—a zero-sum situation. On the other hand, if I have ten units of love and unconditionally give you five, I will feel like I have more love and so will you because love works that way—a non-zero-sum situation.

When a couple is getting along well, they have a lot of non-zero-sum interactions. The more they have, the better they get along, and the better they get along, the more of these interactions they have.

When a couple is not getting along, their relationship can quickly devolve into a zero-sum situation. The relationship becomes transactional. They may accuse each other of "keeping score." The more committed they are to a zero-sum stance, the more fear, anger, and resentment they generate in themselves and each other.

Ironically, the only way out of this devolving spiral is for one partner to unilaterally adopt a non-zero-sum stance. If both decide to do this, all the better.

Adopting a non-zero-sum stance in a zero-sum circumstance is not easy. Even if you see it as the good and right thing to do, it can feel unnatural and self-defeating, even painful. What helps is to value what your partner needs and what the relationship needs more than what you need.

To illustrate:

Cameron and Elaine are at an impasse. Much to Cameron's chagrin, they've accumulated substantial debt. Determined to pay off the debt, Cameron is looking for a second job. Elaine is more comfortable with the debt and resents Cameron's taking a second job because it reduces the time they have together. Cameron believes her well-being depends on reducing debt. Elaine believes her well-being depends on time spent together with her partner. Both are caught in zero-sum thinking around two basic resources: time and money.

If they were to approach the issue from a non-zero-sum perspective focusing on each other's needs, Cameron might say, "I get that you'd like us to have more time together. I would too! Let's have a conversation about how we can cut expenses and maybe create some income together." Or Elaine might say, "I can see how debt makes you anxious. Let's both look for short-term part-time jobs so we can pay things off. Taking care of the debt will feel better to me if we are doing it together."

If they shifted that focus to what the relationship needs, their priority would be their connection even as they talk about their differences. The need for a solution would be secondary to being in the situation together. Taking this stance often changes how a couple feels about a conflict and how they view its resolution.

For example, Cameron might say, "Now that I know you understand my perspective, I feel like you're more with me than against me. I don't have the same urgency about getting a second job. I'm sure we can address the debt and still feel good about each other."

The non-zero-sum approach often produces an unexpected and typically positive result.

CONSIDER THIS...

The more you keep score, the more immersed you are in a zero-sum relationship.

Merging and Separating

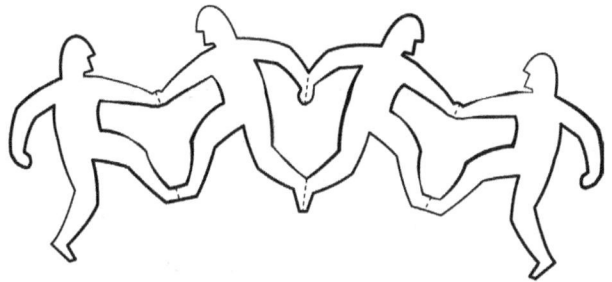

Bob: "I love being with Amanda. We get along great whether we're doing a project together or just sitting on the deck reading. I love when she texts me asking how soon I'll be home. That coming-together moment at the end of the day is a favorite."

Amanda: "I love being with Bob. He's so easygoing and understanding. When I want to spend an evening with my friends, he always tells me to have a good time. He never seems jealous or worried. The truth is, he doesn't need to be jealous or worried because he knows I love him, and I look forward to seeing him when I get home."

Bob and Amanda enjoy the rhythm of merging and separating. They enjoy it because they trust the rhythm and each other. When they are physically together, each one trusts it will be okay to separate. When they are separated, each one trusts that the other will want to come together again, and that he or she will be welcomed.

Partners in unhealthy relationships don't trust this rhythm. When merged, they aren't comfortable with separating. When separate, they aren't confident about what will happen when they merge again.

The merging and separating flow is most often disrupted when the two partners' desires are not synchronized.

For example, when the couple is together, one of them refuses to allow a comfortable separation. The root cause is usually fear of loss or disconnection. He or she may be thinking: "I'm enjoying a wonderful feeling of connection right now. I don't want you to leave because I'm not sure we can recreate it."

Or, when they are separated, one of them refuses to seek out or welcome a merging moment. The root cause is usually fear of losing one's self in the relationship. He or she may think: "I'm enjoying the freedom I feel right now. If I give it up in order to merge, I may not get it again."

These patterns are accompanied by ambivalence about the relationship. Unconsciously, one partner is likely thinking, "I'm comfortable moving toward you only if I sense you are moving away." Or "I'm comfortable moving away only when I sense you are moving toward me." It's as if they are connected at the waist by a ten-foot pole; when one takes a step toward the other, the other takes a step back.

When merging and separating are working well, the partners' desires for connection are timed similarly. If one's timing is too different from the other's, merging is random and unpredictable, which can make it difficult to relate comfortably. A simple lack of awareness can produce this pattern.

A thriving relationship includes a constant, predictable pattern of merging and separating. So, notice the choreography of your relationship. If it feels out of sync, perhaps it's time to pay close attention to the timing and intentions of movement between the two of you.

CONSIDER THIS . . .

To comfortably merge and separate
is to trust your partner.

Pursuer
and Distancer

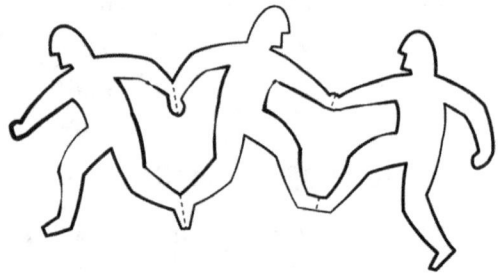

Chuck and Sarah have been together for fifteen years, married for twelve. They met in their early twenties. He used to eat lunch at the diner where she waitressed. She had a way of encouraging conversation without being intrusive, and her openness was an invitation to step outside his usual shyness.

The dance between her openness and his reservation was exciting for both. When Sarah subtly pursued and Chuck responded, she felt powerful and attractive. When he held himself back, he felt strong and mature. She enjoyed the challenge of drawing him out and watching him get to know himself, and her, better. He basked in her attention, noticing how she found his "strong, silent type" attractive. That's why they began seeing each other, and it's why they decided to marry.

For the first few years, the way they complemented each other remained interesting, even exciting. But eventually, Sarah grew tired of being in charge of their emotional connection, of always being the first to say "I love you." All she ever heard was "I love you too." She began feeling resentful, even a bit lonely.

When she began expressing how she felt, Chuck grew confused. From his perspective, life was good. He was focused on his work and his responsibilities around the house, doing what he figured a good husband is supposed to do. Although he was less excited about Sarah's pursuing him emotionally than when they first met, he still enjoyed it. More than that, he'd come to rely on it. Since she was so good at emotional connection, it was one less thing he had to worry about.

Chuck and Sarah were caught in a classic marital pattern: one person pursues while the other distances. It had become exhausting for Sarah and numbing for Chuck. If they kept this up, in a couple years she would run out of steam and he would fall asleep at the wheel.

Because a relationship pattern is often produced through years of repetitive interaction, it can wear a groove into the soul of the marriage. Breaking the pattern requires awareness, effort, patience, and a lot of love.

For instance, the pursuer-distancer pattern is best broken when the pursuer stops pursuing, which is likely to bring on feelings of emptiness, as if he or she has quit a job without having a new one. And the distancer is likely feel abandoned and annoyed. Both will feel confused.

Confusion is usually a sign that genuine change is about to occur. It is exactly what the couple needs to embrace if they are serious about making changes in the relationship.

To break the pursuer-distancer pattern:

- Identify which of you is typically the pursuer and which is the distancer.

- Notice whether these roles shift depending on the topic. For example, does one pursue and the other distance when it comes to work around the house? . . . when it comes to parenting?

- Whichever of you identifies as the pursuer, ask yourself: "What do I fear will happen if I don't pursue?"

- Whichever of you identifies as the distancer, ask yourself: "What do I fear will happen if I stand still, become receptive, and don't distance myself?"

- Share your fears with each other.

Simply engaging in a conversation that includes these points is sometimes enough to break the pursuer-distancer cycle and erode the pattern.

 CONSIDER THIS . . .

As trust diminishes
the pursuer-distancer pattern flourishes.

A Paradox:
Risk and Stability

Embedded in all growth are two mutually dependent elements: risk and stability. Reasonable risk-taking needs a trusted, stable platform from which to launch. Stability needs risk-taking to not grow stagnant.

Here is a simple example. Once a relationship begins to establish itself, it's common for one or the other partner to wonder: What are we to each other? It's a risky question to ask knowing the answer might not be what you hope for. Assuming the answer moves you deeper into the relationship, the outcome of taking the risk needs stability to take root. That is, for the relationship to continue, you need to be steady and reliable.

A new relationship is thrilling precisely because it feels so risky. As it moves forward, it settles into a rhythmic oscillation between risk and stability that keeps it on course. It's when a couple loses the ability to move fluidly between them that problems arise.

Ordinarily, the longer a relationship continues, the more risk averse the couple tends to become, because there's more to lose if a risk taken goes badly. As risk-taking decreases, stability increases. The partners become bored, and the relationship grows flat. "The thrill is gone," to quote B. B. King.

Sometimes risk and stability become polarized—one partner attached to risk, the other to stability—and the flow between them ceases. This can happen around a certain issue.

For example,

> Don grew up in a home where money was tight. He learned early on to be cautious with money, to save what he had so he could have fun later. He became attached to stability. His partner, Tim, was also raised in a home where money was tight, but he learned that to get what he wanted he had to step out and take some risks. In high school, his solution to poverty was to sell weed to classmates (this was before marijuana was legalized in his state). He grew attached to risk. Now, when Don and Tim need to make financial decisions, each sees the other's strategy as a dead end.

Whatever form the loss of fluidity takes, reinstating it can begin with a conversation that acknowledges the importance of both risk and stability. If you find yourself afraid of risk, remember that all movement entails some degree of risk. If you find yourself put off by stability, remember that risk is more likely to achieve its goal if it is rooted in stability.

CONSIDER THIS . . .

Without stability, every risk seems unreasonable.

Why Not
Make It Simple?

Building Blocks for Smooth Relating

Reciprocity

A well-oiled interaction is characterized by give and take. For example, I give you a gift; you smile and say, "Thank you!" Or you help me with a project; I return the favor by asking if there's anything I can do for you. That's all a positive social interaction requires.

A negative social interaction is also reciprocal. For example, I give you the cold shoulder; you give me the silent treatment. Or you find fault in the way I do something; I reply by citing something I don't like about what you do.

Positive reciprocity is essential to a good relationship, especially over the long haul. Sometimes things get in the way of being able to reciprocate, such as physical illness or being apart from each other for a period of time. A well-functioning relationship can usually weather these gaps, if it has been built on a foundation of countless positive reciprocal exchanges.

Sometimes reciprocity shows up as simple politeness—saying "please" and "thank you." Sometimes it shows up in mundane tasks —you wash the dishes and I'll dry them. Sometimes it shows up in more complicated areas like—how you think about and purchase gifts for each other.

Not reciprocating positive behavior usually has consequences. If you spend a lot of time and energy giving yet get little back from your partner, you will likely feel some resentment. If you don't reciprocate your partner's positive behavior adequately, you will likely feel guilty; you're not meeting a basic relationship expectation.

Pay careful attention to how reciprocity is working between you and your partner. If it's going in a positive direction, make sure it continues. If it's going in a negative direction, turn it around by offering something positive and then waiting for your partner to reciprocate.

CONSIDER THIS . . .

Reciprocity is the fuel that powers a relationship.

Congruence
of Perception

For a relationship to run smoothly, the two partners' perceptions of each other need to be congruent—they need to be aligned. When they are not, the effect can be a constant struggle to match those two perceptions.

For instance, if I think I'm a good partner and my wife agrees, we will get along great. But if I think I'm a good partner and she thinks I am failing miserably, we will at best feel disconnected. More likely, I will feel misunderstood, or worse, blamed and disrespected.

It is just as challenging if I think I'm a lousy partner and she thinks I'm doing fine. She will be annoyed by my poor self-image, and I will be annoyed by her inability to see me the way I see myself.

There are two complementary ways to address the incongruity of perception. To continue the example, if I think I'm being a good partner, but my wife sees me as unconcerned with keeping up the house and thus lazy:

I can reevaluate my behavior from her point of view.
I might say,

> "I can see why you think of me as not caring
> about keeping our house nice. I hate yard work and
> prefer to avoid it. So, you're right, I am kind of lazy."

Or she can reevaluate her assessment of me from my point of view. She might reconsider my behavior, noticing things I've done that she'd forgotten about, and readjust her perception of me. She might say,

> "I've been pretty critical of your lack of involvement
> in keeping up the house and yard. But I realize you do
> a lot more than I give you credit for."

Either way, our perceptions will now be congruent.

Congruence of perception underlies even the most mundane exchanges, so it is worth paying attention to. If you and your partner begin an exchange with mutual understanding of each other, what follows is more likely to improve your relationship.

CONSIDER THIS . . .

Your ability to change how you see yourself
and how you see your partner is a measure
of your relationship's health.

Equivalence

In a well-functioning relationship, both partners feel valued for what they bring to the partnership, and each appreciates what the other brings to it. They don't have to bring the same things; those things just need to be valued equivalently. While this sounds like reciprocity, it is different. Reciprocity is about action. Equivalence is about values.

Sorting out the value of each partner's contribution is a task couples must engage in periodically as their relationship changes over time.

A classic example: You might work a full-time job while your partner stays home to care for the house and kids. If each of you sees the value of these very different yet essential contributions as similar, the relationship will feel balanced.

Thus, your respect for what your partner brings to the relationship matters a lot.

If, for some reason, you begin to lose respect for what your partner is offering, you may start sliding into resentment. And if you begin to value your partner's contributions over your own, you might start sliding into guilt.

Similarly, if you value your own contributions to the relationship more highly than you value your partner's, it will be easy to begin to feel resentment. And if you undervalue your contribution, you will likely begin to feel guilty.

To keep guilt and resentment from eroding the quality of your life together, maintain a sense of equivalence. Engage in periodic conversations about what each of you brings to the relationship and the value of those contributions.

CONSIDER THIS . . .

Generously valuing your partner's contributions to the relationship is an expression of love.

Understanding Is Not Enough

When one person is speaking about an event he or she found particularly painful, it's natural for the listener to express understanding: "I understand," "I get it," "I know what you mean."

Here is an example:

Mel: "It hurt to know that you reached out to your brother about what was on your mind before you told me. It was like you don't trust me, like you are closer to your brother than to me, your husband. I have to say that I felt a little betrayed."

Randy: "I get it. You'd like me to come to you with my concerns before I go to anyone else. That would make you feel more important in my life."

This is a "textbook" active listening response, and Randy likely assumes it has assuaged Mel's hurt. But understanding alone doesn't always satisfy. It comes close, but another ingredient is also necessary. That ingredient is appreciation.

When appreciation is also present, "I get it" or "I understand" is followed by a detailed, empathic reflection of the speaker's expressed emotional pain.

Another example:

Randy: "The other night at the party, it really felt crappy when you left me to spend the rest of the evening talking with your friends instead of introducing me to people and making sure I got to know them."

Mel: "I get it. I can see how that would make you feel bad. You'd like me to spend more time with you to make sure you're feeling comfortable. That makes sense, especially when I remember that your parents were rarely there for you and didn't have a clue about how to help you with your shyness."

Mel's reference to Randy's past tells Randy that Mel not only understands what he did but also appreciates how his misstep landed for Randy.

Understanding is the capacity to intellectually grasp the specifics of a situation. Appreciation goes further. It conveys the listener's heartfelt grasp of the situation's meaning for the speaker. We can usually tell when our partner's grasp of what we are expressing is only intellectual and when it goes deeper.

When the situation is personally important, we want our perspective to be both understood and appreciated. The two together create a healing bond that can overcome all kinds of hurt.

CONSIDER THIS . . .
Appreciation gives legs to understanding.

The Need for Control

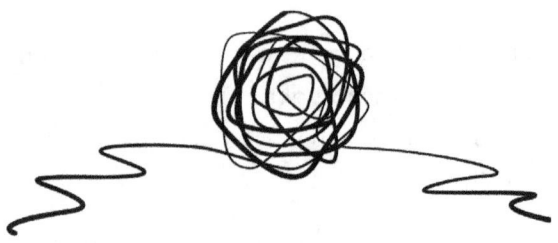

Anna and Ben became a couple in their mid-twenties. She loved the way he took it upon himself to meet her needs. He loved to feel needed, and because Anna always knew what she wanted, how to meet her needs was never a mystery.

For a long time, Anna and Ben enjoyed the sense of control that came with knowing how to please each other, how to initiate good experiences and avoid bad ones. But over time, both began to change—to grow. As their needs and wants shifted, their habitual ways of meeting each other's needs became less reliable. It became harder to start good experiences and stop bad ones, and they both began to feel a loss of control.

Like most couples who experience a good connection slipping through their fingers, Anna and Ben became frightened. Each began to insist that the other notice where needs weren't being met and adopt new ways of responding.

Each felt the other's fear and insistence. The control they enjoyed earlier in their relationship had been borne of love and confidence. The control they now exercised was borne of caution and fear. They began to use the word "control" as an accusation, as if few things could be worse than needing to control.

The truth is, having a certain amount of control over what we experience in a relationship is a basic interpersonal need. When we can make good things happen and stop bad things from happening, we are likely to be happy. When we can't, we feel anxious and unhappy.

For Anna and Ben, an open, problem-solving conversation about needs and desires would help each of them regain a sense of control borne of love and confidence. That conversation could start with acknowledging together the value of having a certain control over one's relationship experience. From there, the conversation could move to identifying times when it has felt good when the other takes control. And times when it has felt good to relinquish control.

CONSIDER THIS ...

When control is held lightly,
it keeps a relationship on track.

Apologies Aren't All They're Cracked Up to Be

Dan: "I'm sorry! I didn't mean to upset you. It was only a joke. Please don't take what I said so seriously."

Tracey: "Well, it was a damn poor joke! The truth is, you've said that kind of thing in the past, and it sure as hell wasn't a joke then."

Dan: "Yeah, I know. I thought we were in a better place. I thought we could be a little playful about stuff that used to cause a lot of arguing. I'm really sorry! Can't you just accept my apology and let it go?"

Tracey: "No! I can't just let it go. It hit too close to home. This is stuff I still have a hard time forgetting."

Dan: "Jeez! Again, I'm sorry...."

Dan screwed up. He created a painful experience that Tracey can't let go of. He's apologized several times, and Tracey knows he's sincere. Yet she can't accept the apology and move on. Why is that?

An apology is important, even essential. But unless the infraction is trivial, it doesn't wrap up what happened and tie a neat bow around it so it can be aside.

An apology simply opens the door.

It elicits permission for a deeper, more healing conversation to follow. It's a bit like calling your physician when you're sick. The call is only the first step. The visit and examination are where recovery takes place.

Once an apology has opened the door, the hard work can begin. Healing is a process—sometimes a long one. Your job as the offender is to initiate that process and follow it through to the end. This means taking the additional step of letting the offended person know you appreciate how the hurt landed in his or her life and the ripple effects it might have generated.

For example, Dan might say: "I'm sorry I made you the butt of a joke. I was only kidding. I know your dad used to belittle you in front of your friends, and what I said must have felt a lot like that. It had to have hurt."

CONSIDER THIS . . .

An apology is just the beginning of a conversation.

Don't Take
It Personally

Think of the times you or your partner has made a statement like

"What did you mean by that?"

Or...

"I can't believe you actually think such a thing about me!"

Comments like these show that you've been snagged by the belief that your partner is doing something to you. You feel attacked, so you instinctively defend yourself.

I learned this for myself during a fight with my wife years ago. She began describing, in uncomfortable detail, all the ways I had failed her and disappointed her. Naturally, I took offense and began to defend myself. I had gotten out just a few sentences when she stopped me and said, "Why is it that every time we have this discussion it always has to be about you?"

The question took the wind right out of my sails and left me confused. She was talking about my behavior, so how was it *not* about me?

That exchange didn't resolve itself immediately. We stumbled to an acceptable conclusion. It then took some serious reflection to see that my attention in that moment needed to have been on her feelings, not on my feelings and my self-defense. Yes, I had done things she didn't like, but more important than the specifics of my wrongs was the fact that she was hurt and disappointed. She needed me to hear that and to meet her there.

Eventually, I said to myself, "You mean this wasn't about me? You mean I don't have to take this personally? You mean my job is to simply hear, understand, and accept her disappointment?"

I learned a lot from that exchange with my wife, including how strongly we are inclined to take things personally, to be reactive and defend ourselves. It takes a lot of practice, as well as a deep desire to be present with our partner, to hear things we'd rather not hear with genuineness and compassion instead.

Just imagine the freedom of knowing you can share with your partner your disappointment in him or her without needing to be ready to duck once the words pass your lips. The two of you would likely feel closer and, paradoxically, a lot less disappointed in each other.

CONSIDER THIS . . .

To take something personally is to value what's happening to you over what's happening in your relationship.

A Paradox:
Freedom and Limits

The tension between freedom and limits is built right into life. Our sojourn on earth is limited by time—we live only so long—and we are free to make of that time what we want. We are limited by circumstance or resources, and we are free to choose how we respond to those conditions.

The freedom-limits dialogue sits at the core of how a couple relates to each other. It may even have been elemental in their attraction to each other.

It seems we come into the world hardwired for either fear of freedom or fear of limits. If we're wired to fear freedom, we will be attracted to someone who isn't afraid of it. Their ease with risk-taking will feel like a breath of fresh air. If we're wired to fear limits, we will be attracted to someone who is comfortable with them. Their ease with structure will feel grounding and stable.

Under sufficient stress, however, we typically retreat to our basic instincts and start to see even the mildest version of its opposite as a threat. For example, when stressed financially, the partner who fears freedom will see minor, necessary spending as a threat to security, while the partner who fears limits will experience a restricted budget as smothering—as if they are being choked to death. The conflict that follows will have all the qualities of a life-and-death struggle. The purchase of a pair of inexpensive flip-flops can ignite an all-out battle.

Recognizing the role and impact of the freedom-limits paradox can go a long way toward not only managing conflict but making it productive. By attending to the fear experienced instead of to the topic that arouses the fear (e.g., whether to purchase a pair of flip-flops) a couple can address the root cause of the disagreement and thereby perhaps prevent future disagreements.

CONSIDER THIS . . .

Fluid movement between valuing limits and valuing freedom is a marker of a healthy relationship.

Why Not Experiment?

Five Relationship Skills to Explore

The Skill of
Not Asking Questions

Questions are a natural way to find out what you need or want to know, but they aren't the only way. Sometimes not asking a question is the better approach.

Asking for information that simply helps life move along is rarely a problem. For example,

"Have you seen my keys?"

"When are we supposed to be at the meeting?"

"How many eggs do you want for breakfast?"

But sometimes we want information about deeper matters—about aspects of an exchange that aren't all that obvious. Asking for deeper information is fair. However, in this context a question can come across as a threat, prompting defensiveness in the person being questioned. For example,

"Who were you talking to on the phone?"

"Why don't you want to go to the party with me?"

"What did you mean when you said you were
too busy to help me?"

Instead, make a statement that shares your perspective and invites your partner to say more. For example,

"I get that you are really busy, but I'm a little confused
by your reluctance to give me a hand. Help me understand."

"I notice that you're on your phone a lot lately. It makes
me a little nervous. I know it's probably not a big deal,
but it will help me feel more comfortable if you share
a little something about your calls."

"I can imagine several good reasons you don't want
to go to the party. I'd love to hear your thoughts
about the whole thing."

A statement that reveals what's true for you coupled with an expressed desire to hear your partner's perspective offers openness and invites conversation.

CONSIDER THIS . . .

Gathering information without asking a question
is an exercise in love.

The Skill of Asking Permission

When you've been in a relationship for a while, it's natural to take for granted things that appear to never change, like your partner's perspective on going out for happy hour on Friday nights. But in some contexts, it's better not to take things for granted.

For example, instead of assuming your partner is always ready for a serious conversation, ask his or her permission before opening that kind of discussion.

> "Would it be okay with you if we had a talk
> about how we spend money?"

Or...

> "I'd like to have a conversation about how we parent.
> Would that be okay with you?"

Asking for and receiving permission has three important benefits.

- First, it conveys respect. And respect (even more than love) is the foundation of a successful relationship.

- Second, it lets your partner know that you value him or her and respect his or her time and energy.

- Third, if your partner gives permission, it means he or she has bought into whatever happens next and is therefore a willing participant. This goes a long way toward ensuring you will have a constructive conversation.

CONSIDER THIS . . .
Moving forward without your partner's
consent rarely ends well.

The Skill of the Excellent Hug

Some couples are naturally good at hugging. Others not so much. For those who are naturally good at it, the following are a few reminders. For those who find a good hug hard to pull off, try these suggestions:

- **Make it face to face.** While a side-by-side hug or a from-the-back hug can be nice, a genuine hug is face to face and toe to toe.

- **Make it steady and grounding.** An excellent hug does not include patting and rubbing, which can signal discomfort, anxiety, or even condescension and can also make it difficult for your partner to relax into the hug. Just stand there and hold your partner with no agenda other than to just be present with him or her.

- **Keep it nonsexual.** There's clearly a time for sexual hugging, but most of the time people, even intimate partners, just want to be held. There is no other intention besides the experience of comfort, support, and love.

- **Make it last a little longer—at least thirty seconds.** An excellent hug is a little longer than a greeting hug. It communicates that you accept your partner and want to spend time with him or her. It lasts long enough to let the person know you are comfortable with yourself and with him or her.

- **With your intimate partner, give hugs freely and frequently.** An excellent hug comes with no expectation beyond the hug itself.

- **Make it full body.** There's the "A" hug where the two people lean in from the top but don't allow the rest of their bodies to touch. And there's the "H" hug where only arms are involved—no body contact. There are times for both kinds of hugs. But an excellent hug involves total body contact.

- **Make sure it's mutual.** There is certainly a place and time for a one-way hug, but a truly excellent hug is mutual. Both parties are in it 100 percent.

CONSIDER THIS . . .

Regular thirty-second hugs may be all that's required for a harmonious relationship.

The Skill of the Excellent Kiss

From the anxiety-ridden first kiss of adolescents to the symbolic "You may kiss the bride" to the ritual peck as a couple parts company, kissing offers intimate partners the opportunity to demonstrate desire, support, care, commitment, and presence. There are all kinds of kisses. Here are three to serve as starters.

- **The ritual kiss** happens at designated times, usually times of transition. There's the kiss when you transition from wakefulness to sleep—the goodnight kiss. The kiss when you transition from together to apart—the goodbye kiss. The kiss when you meet—the welcome home kiss. Ritual kisses speak to the important "ordinariness" of a stable, steady connection.

- **The lingering/testing kiss** happens when you want to see where you and your partner are with each other. It's probably the one that requires the most courage and vulnerability. It reaches out and offers interest, and maybe desire. It's an invitation, and like all invitations, it comes with the risk of rejection. It may be the most important kind of kiss.

- **The erotic/sexual kiss.** Most of us know this kiss from movies and books if not from experience. It's the one that says, "I'm all in!" It's unreserved, passionate, and complete. It's also playful and open. It's the one that turns having sex into lovemaking.

Pay attention to kissing. There are few easily accessed experiences better than giving and receiving a well-timed, well-chosen kiss.

CONSIDER THIS . . .
Few things are more intimate than
a 6-second, non-pucker kiss.

The Skill of Encouraging Curiosity

Recall the early stages of your relationship—how hungry you were to know every little thing about your partner. You were curious about his/her past and future. Curious about his/her body. Curious also about yourself in relationship to him/her. Because everything about your connection with this person was new, curiosity came naturally.

As a relationship matures, new and interesting information about each other is harder to come by. It requires an attentive ear, a watchful eye, and a good dose of determination to keep the flame of curiosity alive.

Curiosity is a skill that can be deliberately cultivated.

Imagine, for example, overhearing a phone conversation between your partner and an unknown caller that raises questions in your mind. Whether you approach that situation with curiosity or suspicion largely determines the quality of that interaction. Even if you feel anxious in that moment, it is possible, and productive, to set that aside and let curiosity lead.

Think of curiosity as a muscle. If exercised, it gets stronger and more responsive. Left alone, it will atrophy and become useless. Exercised curiosity keeps a relationship fresh and alive. Here are some suggestions for encouraging curiosity.

- Odd as it might seem, simply using the word more frequently can be helpful. For example, "I'm curious about how your meeting went today." Or "I'm curious about your thoughts on our finances." Naming your curiosity sets the stage for an open conversation.

- Judgment diminishes curiosity. Allow yourself to wonder without judgment why you do what you do and why your partner does what he/she does.

- When you and your partner are doing simple problem-solving (e.g., what to make for dinner or how to decorate a room), invite him/her to offer options as a way of demonstrating your curiosity about your partner's preferences.

- When your partner suggests options, take a little time to experience curiosity about his/her ideas before deciding on a next step.

CONSIDER THIS . . .
Without curiosity, intimacy withers.

What Do You See When You Step Back?

Perspectives That Sustain a Relationship

Attending to the Whole of Your Relationship

Why is dessert served at the end of a meal? Why not at the beginning or in the middle?

While there may be gustatory reasons for serving dessert last, a psychological reason is that we tend to evaluate an experience in terms of how it ended. A few bites of sweetness at the end can remedy the impression of a mediocre meal.

That said, when we define an entire experience by how it ends, we risk underappreciating the full experience. This is very much true with relationships.

 Joe and Rachel usually have a hectic morning getting themselves ready for work and their children ready for school. This morning went particularly well with both willingly addressing the getting-out-of-the-door tasks. During the day they exchanged supportive and informative texts, even mentioning how well the morning routine had gone. On the way home, however, Joe grew irritated having run into heavy traffic that delayed him by half an hour. By the time he walked through the door, Rachel was frazzled by the children's demands. It wasn't long before Joe and Rachel were taking their frustrations out on each other.

What had begun as an unusually good day was ruined by heavy traffic and the demands of parenting.

In the best-case scenario, after the children are in bed, Joe and Rachel will take some time to connect. They will recall their difficult end-of-the-day reunion and remind themselves of the good feelings they had through most of the day.

Periodically reviewing their relationship and the satisfaction level each of them experiences can be eye-opening for a couple. An easy way to do this is to use the financial analyst's approach for reviewing a company's annual income: looking at each quarter and identifying its main theme to track the company's growth. For instance, you might see that the first quarter of your relationship was particularly difficult, followed by a healing quarter, then an uneventful quarter, and most recently a quarter of renewed challenges, revealing the evolution of your relationship.

Ritual moments, such as anniversaries, are natural occasions for reflecting on and savoring the whole of your relationship's history. New Year's Day is a wonderful time to look back on the good and difficult moments in the past year. A midlife crisis, challenging though it may be, often demands that partners acknowledge their relationship history, put past events into perspective, and chart a mutually acceptable way forward.

Taking time to sit down together and assess your relationship lets you and your partner note strengths and weaknesses as well as the rhythm in which they show up. Essentially, it offers a wholistic perspective on your life together. This may require some vulnerability and courage if it brings up painful times. Yet it can also be an opportunity to grieve and let go of those events or implement healing strategies, even as you acknowledge and celebrate the good times.

CONSIDER THIS . . .

Regularly and jointly assessing your relationship is the preventive maintenance it needs for a long, healthy lifespan.

Grounding Yourself in the Present Moment

Sandy and Steve have just made love. Not just any old love, but really connected, deeply felt and enjoyed love. As Sandy lies on her back enjoying the moment she starts thinking about how long it has been since they last made love like that. Steve looks lovingly at Sandy and starts wondering when making love like that will happen again. She's half in the past, and he's half in the future. Neither is fully in the present.

While making love like that, they had to have been fully present with each other. That presence, however, evaporated when her attention turned to the past and his to the future. By slipping out of the present moment, they lost that precious togetherness that they could have taken with them into the remainder of the day.

Ideally, Sandy and Steve are able to notice their minds wandering and choose to bring themselves back to the moment. It can be helpful to do this out loud, one or both partners speaking their effort to remain present, thus making it part of their mutual experience.

Remaining in the present is as relevant in difficult times as it is in times of connection. When conflicts arise, the ability to stay with what's happening here and now, not referencing similar conflicts in the past or projecting conflict into the future, can determine how productively the conflict is resolved.

The capacity to stay grounded in the present moment may be one of the clearest indicators of intimate partners' ability to fully experience good times and successfully navigate challenges together.

CONSIDER THIS . . .

Not getting distracted by the past or the future is the key to unlocking togetherness in the present.

Embracing What Comes Next

While being fully present to your partner means being present in *this* moment, life always implies a next step. We are continuously asked to consider the future from the perspective of the here and now. An ever-present example is the relationship between inhaling and exhaling. A completed exhalation implies an inhalation to follow. A completed inhalation implies an exhalation to follow. When they stop implying each other, we are dead—or close to it.

The forward movement of our lives depends on this rhythmic oscillation, and the same is true for a well-functioning relationship. The two partners respond to each other by oscillating between merging and separating. Coming together implies an eventual separation, and separation implies an eventual coming together.

So also, a well-functioning conversation is rhythmic. One partner's speaking implies the other's listening, and one's listening implies the other's speaking.

Connection is a dynamic, reciprocating process in which the present always implies a next step. That step can be as mundane as deciding to make dinner together. When a couple is operating optimally, decision-making and cooperation are a well-choreographed dance, each partner fluidly responding to the other. What should we make? When should we eat? Do we need to go shopping? Who's in charge?

For a couple in a relationship that's growing, little forks in the road like these are navigated handily. For a couple in conflict, the process will, at best, feel rough and awkward. At worst, it will leave them both feeling stuck.

The implied next step can also involve a large-scale, life-changing decision. Should we have a child? Should we buy a house? Should one or the other of us change jobs? Conversations about important choices like these are most productive when they move smoothly from one partner's ideas to the other partner's response, offering and responding, back and forth.

Embracing a next step initiates reflection about that step as well as consideration of the implied step that follows. Awareness and acceptance of what one moment implies for the next is what creates an excellent relationship dance.

CONSIDER THIS . . .

Like driving a car, moving forward in a relationship involves paying attention to what's before and behind you while remaining seated firmly in the present moment.

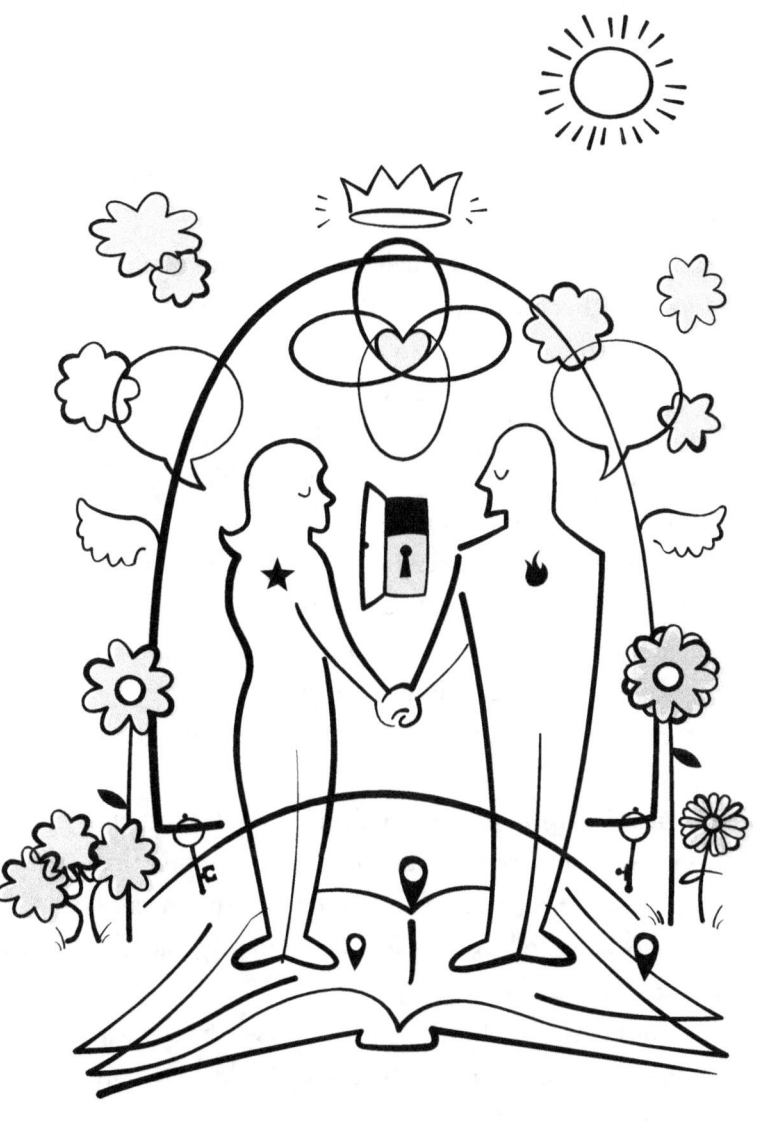

Afterword

For at least two decades, I've wondered if it's possible to present in writing the stunningly complex nature of intimate relationships without boring the reader to death. This little book is an attempt to do just that.

Each essay illuminates a small facet of relating intimately. All the essays together are meant to offer you a better understanding of the whole of intimate connection.

Which raises the question "What is the conceptual foundation I've used for drawing the facets of relating together to create a whole?" The short answer is a synergistic combination of existential philosophy and systems theory.

Existentialism emphasizes individual freedom, choice, and responsibility. When applied to romantic relationships, it encourages the two partners to embrace their autonomy while fostering authentic connection between them.

Here are six ways existentialism relates to couples:

Authentic relating. Existentialism promotes authenticity, urging individuals to be true to themselves rather than conform to societal expectations. In a relationship, this means both partners strive to be genuine rather than play roles dictated by tradition or family.

Authentic love for the other arises when each partner accepts him/herself and feels accepted by the other, flaws, fears, and aspirations included.

Freedom and responsibility. Existentialists argue that individuals are radically free and that with freedom comes responsibility. Consequently, people are responsible for their actions and choices. Applied to relationships, this means each partner freely and actively chooses to commit to the other, rather than relying on external forces such as cultural norms and obligations to bring them together.

As each partner takes responsibility for his or her role in the relationship, he or she is less likely to blame circumstances or the other person when times are difficult.

Commitment as a continuous choice. Existentialists reject the idea of commitment as once and done. Instead, they see it as a continuous act of choice and engagement.

Rather than viewing love and commitment as passive experiences, existentialism suggests that maintaining a deep connection requires ongoing effort, conversation, and conscious decisions.

The angst of love. Existentialism proposes that intimate relationships are plagued by angst—an abiding fear of abandonment, of not being enough, or of losing one's individuality.

In a healthy relationship, that angst is acknowledged but not allowed to dictate actions. Couples who embrace an existential point of view accept the uncertainty inherent in partnership even while they build trust and security.

Interdependence without loss of self. While existentialism values independence, it does not advocate isolation. In an intimate relationship, the two partners can be interdependent—deeply connected while still maintaining their individuality.

Love should not lead to one person losing himself or herself in the other. Instead, partners should challenge and support each other's personal growth.

Confronting mortality together. A core theme in existentialism is awareness of mortality. A quiet and mutual mindfulness of the fleeting nature of life and of endings, including death, can deepen a couple's bond.

Rather than taking each other for granted, an existential couple understands that every moment offers a choice to be present and to engage with one's beloved.

From an existential perspective, love is about neither fairy tale illusions nor absolute certainty. It is about two individuals who choose each other freely, take responsibility for their relationship, and embrace the complexities of human connection. While existentialism acknowledges the difficulties and anxieties of love, it ultimately encourages couples to live meaningfully and authentically together.

While existential philosophy offers a perspective on how individuals might experience themselves in relationship, systems theory speaks to the choreography of individuals relating to each other.

Systems theory was developed in the mid-twentieth century to explain and predict the interdependence of components in natural, technological, and social settings. When applied to relationships, systems theory, while acknowledging the importance of the two individuals, elevates what happens between them above what happens within each of them.

Here are four pillars of systems theory as applied to intimate relationships:

Interdependence. When a couple functions as a system, the relationship is greater than the sum of the two individuals. Each partner's thoughts, emotions, and behaviors are {recognized as occurring not in isolation but} as affecting the other's thoughts, emotions and behaviors.

Circular causality. Problems in the relationship are never caused by just one person. They always arise through mutual influence.

Homeostasis. Couples tend to develop stable interaction patterns, whether these are healthy or unhealthy. When one person changes, the system may resist the change in order to maintain homeostasis (balance and stability). If the one-person change persists, however, maintaining homeostasis will require the system as a whole to change.

Boundaries. In a successful relationship, the two partners have clear yet flexible boundaries. They balance their separateness and their relatedness. In an unsuccessful relationship, the partners tend to have either rigid or very porous boundaries.

Combined, existentialism, with its focus on individual authenticity, and systems theory, with its focus on interdependence, offer a comprehensive framework for grasping and working with the intricacies of intimate relationships.

Why am I bringing all this up at the end of the book?

Because I don't presume the essays you've just read comprise the totality of what's possible or important for you and your partner. Each couple is unique, so the range of wants, needs, and demands of couple life can be infinite.

I want to leave room for you to add your own thoughts to those in this book, to discover the tiny shifts that work especially well for you and your partner. As you come up with your own tiny shifts, it will serve you well if they fall within the framework of existentialism and systems theory You may even want to put them in writing.

Life is chaotic enough. Let's at least maintain a useful framework for how we relate with our intimate partner.

My best to you . . .

Acknowledgments

As an English major in college, I fancied myself a decent writer. What I've learned through the process of creating this little book is that though I might possess the raw material necessary for competent writing, I have a long way to go before I can claim "good writer" status.

I want to thank developmental editor Carolyn Bond, who kindly and gently transformed my raw material into something I can feel proud of. She's been an exceptional shepherd. I'm grateful to her editorial cohort, Sharron Dorr, who was instrumental in shaping the trajectory of my manuscript. I want to also thank Robinson Smith, my illustrator and friend, who has effectively applied his creative talents to my ideas. Conversations with him have illuminated these concepts in ways he will likely never know. Thanks to Kris Weber, an amazingly creative book designer, and Martha Bullen, marketing genius, this little book is now "seeing the light of day," all dressed up and ready to meet the world.

More personally, I want to thank my three children, Rachel, Anna, and Andrew, each of whom in their own unique way has taught me to appreciate the complexity of family life. Finally, thank you, Nicolee Hiltz, for joining me for the remaining chapters of my life.

About the Author

Jake Thiessen, PhD, is a seasoned therapist with over forty-five years of experience helping couples navigate the choppy waters of contemporary relationship life. He has a master's degree in theology with a concentration in marriage and family therapy from Fuller Theological Seminary and a doctorate in family studies from Texas Tech University. For fifteen years he was a university professor teaching courses in marriage and family at Messiah University. Before graduate school he studied at the University of Grenoble, Grenoble, France, and taught English as a second language on an oasis in the Algerian Sahara. His extensive academic and experiential background informs his approach to improving the lives of couples who seek to better relate to each other.

Jake was raised in a tiny town on the Kansas plains where everyone knew everyone and most of their business. The spaciousness of the plains coupled with the enmeshment of that community made him curious about connection and separation, the two essential features of relationship dynamics.

In terms of personal relationship experience, Jake is father to three grown children. He has also navigated a divorce, the death of a spouse, and the dynamics of family expansion with stepchildren, a foster child, and the arrival of grandchildren and great-grandchildren.

He lives in Camp Hill, Pennsylvania, with his current partner, Nicolee Hiltz, PhD, a psychologist who enthusiastically supports his endeavors including writing this book.

To learn more or contact Jake, visit www.jakethiessen.com.

About the Illustrator

Robinson Smith is an illustrator, designer, and full-time creative director working in marketing and advertising. He uses his work to share ideas, tell stories, and communicate with viewers on behalf of his clients.

Robinson was raised in central Pennsylvania, where he continues to live and work. He attended Pennsylvania State University, where he earned a bachelor's degree in graphic design. Over the past thirty years, his work has garnered local, regional, and national recognition and has been published in a number of design periodicals and annuals.

To learn more about Robinson's work, visit RobinsonSmithCreative.com.